INHERITANCE OF TEARS

Trusting the Lord of Life When Death Visits the Womb

Jessalyn Hutto
Cruciform Press | March 2015

For Richard,
I love you with all my heart and am so glad
to have you by my side on this journey heavenward.

CruciformPress

© 2015 by Jessalyn Hutto. All rights reserved.
CruciformPress.com | info@CruciformPress.com

"Miscarriage places women in a secret club that nobody wants to join, but many find themselves in. Because of the nature of the loss, many women grasp for hope in the overwhelming days of grief that follow. I have twice been that woman, and Jessalyn Hutto has written the book I wish I'd had as I walked through the pain of our miscarriages. Filled with Scripture, empathy, and rock-solid hope that God is a good and all-loving Father, this book will be a healing balm to grieving women in your local church."

Courtney Reissig, author, *The Accidental Feminist: Restoring Our Delight in God's Good Design* (Crossway)

"This book is equally important for those who have suffered miscarriage and those who have not. Rarely is the topic of miscarriage addressed with such candor and depth. Deeply personal and brave, *Inheritance of Tears* unveils a picture of miscarriage drawn from first-hand experience and attentive consideration of Scripture. Jessalyn invites us to ask the hard questions, to enter into the suffering of our sisters, to remember the goodness of God even in the midst of unspeakable loss. May her words minister to many."

Jen Wilkin, author, *Women of the Word* (Crossway)

"Miscarriage? Don't talk about it. Sadly, this is the approach many churches take. As a result, the woman in the pew suffers unbearable pain and grieves all alone. Change must happen, and Inheritance of Tears is the place to start. Speaking from firsthand experience, Jessalyn Hutto compassionately wipes the tears from the desolate woman's eyes so that she can see the insurmountable love and unbreakable sovereignty of her Savior, Jesus Christ."

Matthew Barrett, Executive Editor, *Credo Magazine*; Assistant Prof. of Christian Studies, California Baptist U.

"Jessalyn Hutto invites you to experience God's goodness in the midst of your suffering. Having walked through the sorrow of miscarriage, my heart resonates with Jessalyn's bittersweet journey. Jessalyn doesn't back away from the tough questions that loss brings, but offers biblical counsel for the hurting as one who understands their pain. *Inheritance of Tears: Trusting the Lord of Life When Death Visits The Womb* is a personal word of truth and comfort that I highly recommend."

Kimberly Wagner, author, *Fierce Women: The Power of a Soft Warrior* (Moody)

"This is a needed resource for those struggling to know God in the midst of their suffering. Without a solid theological framework, God's role in our suffering is hard to navigate. Jessalyn gives the needed resources to know in truth the God of All Comfort, for only from that foundation can we receive his deep rest in the midst of pain."

Wendy Alsup, author, *Practical Theology for Women: How Knowing God Makes a Difference in Our Daily Lives*

"The pain of miscarriages is grievous and profound. Jessalyn Hutto helps us think about this matter personally, sharing her own anguish and pain. At the same time, she guides us theologically, so that we see God's wisdom, God's purpose, and God's love in the midst of our suffering. I gladly recommend this work to others."

Tom Schreiner, Professor of New Testament Interpretation, The Southern Baptist Theological Seminary

"If you are suffering, I'm so glad you are holding this book. You won't find soggy counsel, glib advice, or verses ripped out of context to make the author's point. Jessalyn writes with warmth, conviction, and clarity, helping us stare down suffering by directing our gaze to the Lord of glory. I think you, and thousands of other women, will be helped by this wonderful book."

JA Medders, author; *Gospel Formed: Living a Grace-Addicted, Truth-Filled, Jesus-Exalting Life* (Kregel)

Cruciform Press

<u>Our Books:</u> Short and to the point—about 100 pages. Clear. Concise. Helpful. Inspiring. Easy to read. Solid authors. Gospel-focused. Local-church oriented.

<u>Website Discounts:</u>

Print Books (list price $9.99)

1-5 Books	$8.45 each
6-50 Books	$7.45 each
More than 50 Books	$6.45 each

Ebooks (list price $7.50)

Single Ebooks	$5.45 each
Bundles of 7 Ebooks	$35.00
Ebook Distribution Program	6 pricing levels

<u>Subscription Options:</u> If you choose, print books or ebooks delivered to you on a schedule, at a discount.

Print Book Subscription *(list $9.99)*	$6.49 each
Ebook Subscription *(list $7.50)*	$3.99 each

Inheritance of Tears: Trusting the Lord of Life When Death Visits the Womb

Print / PDF ISBN: 978-1-941114-01-8
ePub ISBN: 978-1-941114-03-2
Mobipocket ISBN: 978-1-941114-02-5

Table of Contents

Introduction
STORIES

My first exposure to the sorrow of miscarriage was watching my dear friend and youth pastor's wife, Chelle, navigate her way through its murky waters. Then sixteen years old, I had recently put my trust in Jesus for salvation, and Chelle had become my spiritual mentor. Though she and her husband had been blessed with three beautiful girls, they had also experienced two tragic miscarriages. During my time under their ministry, they faced a third heartbreaking loss.

Week after week, Chelle had poured her passion for the Word of God into me, teaching me what a life devoted to Christ should look like. Suddenly, all of that theory was being lived out before my eyes. What Chelle actually believed about the Lord and his Word was on display for all to see. As her young disciple in the faith, I took in every tearful smile she passed on to me. Her testimony of trust in the Lord's good providence was a lesson in practical theology I could never have learned from a book. At the time, I had no idea how important and applicable those lessons would be for my future.

Heartbreak in Black and White

In the spring of 2008, while my husband, Richard, was attending seminary in Louisville, Kentucky, I discovered I was pregnant with our first baby. While he was gone for the day, I painstakingly planned how I would reveal the wonderful news. That evening, we enjoyed a delicious dinner, followed by a cake iced in baby blue and pink. We then sat down to a favorite Jimmy Stewart movie in which his character's wife also plans a special announcement.

At the moment Stewart's character learns they are pregnant with their first child, I handed Richard a gift. He quickly opened it to find a figurine I had seen him admiring in a store only weeks earlier—a man cradling a baby in his arms. As I confirmed his elated guess, joy filled our one-bedroom apartment and we celebrated, dreaming of the infant we would soon hold close.

Those particular dreams never came to pass. Just weeks later, even before our first doctor's appointment, I began cramping and bleeding. I hoped and prayed that these symptoms were not signs of miscarriage, but after an ultrasound there was little room for optimism. The baby's tiny form was there, but the reassuring sound of a heartbeat was missing. I was sent home with a fuzzy black-and-white image of our baby and the simple instructions to "see what would happen." I was told that my body might expel the "tissue" naturally, in which case there would be no need for medical intervention.

My husband and I left the doctor's office stunned and filled with dread. Over the next two days, my cramping and bleeding intensified. Horrible contractions came and went until their regularity and intensity signaled there was no turning back. Finally, in one terrible moment it was over. Any sliver of hope hidden in the depths of my heart had vanished.

Our baby's life had slipped from my body, and the grief was overwhelming. I emerged from our bathroom to tell my husband and mother. We cried and prayed, seeking comfort from the only one who could provide it. My husband lifted up his quivering voice, praising the Lord for his goodness and love, thanking him for the gift of the precious life I had carried, and then expressing our rekindled longing for our Savior's return. Indeed, that coming day when sin and death will be no more had never seemed so precious.

But this is far from the end of our story. In the coming years, our family size doubled as the Lord blessed us with two healthy, beautiful baby boys. My body seemed to be handling pregnancy well now, and my fears of miscarrying again lessened with each of those two births. So, as Richard and I sat in the waiting room for the seventeen-week doctor's appointment for my fourth pregnancy, I pushed aside any thoughts of complications and chose to focus on the upcoming ultrasound. Soon we would find out whether we'd be adding a third little boy to our growing family or our first little girl.

After what seemed like an eternity, we were taken to an examination room. Following the usual pattern, the nurse began by checking our baby's heartbeat. She slowly slid the ultrasound wand from one side of my belly to the other, but all we could hear was empty static. Seconds turned into agonizing minutes without a single reassuring thump, and the nurse asked a technician to help get a clearer picture of what was happening inside my womb. It took him only seconds of looking at the ultrasound monitor to conform that our little one, a girl, had died. Her life had come to an abrupt halt at about fifteen weeks' gestation and our worst nightmare had come true.

The horror of this discovery was debilitating. As we looked in disbelief at the image of our lifeless baby girl on that grainy black-and-white screen, great sobs escaped our lips. Now we would have to make the difficult decisions associated with a second-trimester miscarriage. I grasped my swollen tummy and lay back on the examination table, waiting for the doctor to come explain what we might do next. After hearing our options, we decided to induce labor in a couple of days.

I spent the next forty-eight hours begging God for a miracle. I couldn't wrap my mind around the concept of my baby girl's body resting lifelessly within my womb. How desperately I wanted to feel her move! How I hoped the technician had missed something or made some kind of mistake! As I prayed to the Lord through painful, gut-wrenching sobs seeking to accept his perfect will, the Holy Spirit graciously allowed me to experience a peace only he can give. By his grace, though the grief was overwhelming, I was not overcome. Though the reality of what had occurred seemed altogether too painful to accept, my soul rested upon our holy God's perfect and good providence. His presence was very real and near to us during those terrible days.

When we finally held our little girl in our hands and viewed her perfect, tiny frame, we praised God for such a gracious gift. Though her life had been measured in mere weeks, the blessings we received from it would be impossible to number. We named her Anastasia, which means "resurrection."

An Unseen Grief

In our post-fall world, sin and death affect every facet of our lives. This terrible reality means that many pregnancies will end in sorrow rather than joy. Yet this specific type of loss, which is so overwhelmingly common, is rarely addressed from the pulpit—or even by women's ministries. Many couples choose not to share their loss with their church body due to its extremely personal nature. I believe this unfortunately perpetuates the false notion that miscarriages are both uncommon and easily worked through. As women try to navigate the horror of their babies dying within them, they are often left with little biblical counsel to draw from.

After experiencing my first miscarriage, a whole new world of suffering in the church opened up to me. Suddenly I became aware of the many women going through similar trials—whether infertility, miscarriage, or stillbirth. It seemed that no matter where I looked, women were silently dealing with terrible losses. Even today as I type these words, I have two dear friends who've recently lost their babies. Although few share such stories beyond a small circle, the truth is that miscarriages are shockingly common.

Having experienced this sorrow myself and grieved alongside my sisters in Christ as they've walked through it, I've become increasingly convinced that the church desperately needs a solid theological framework with which to make sense of this suffering. Women don't need empty platitudes or frivolous advice when their babies die: they need God and his Word! When crippled by such bewildering pain, suffering couples need truth to stand upon. They need fellow believers equipped to come alongside them in their time of grief—friends who understand their sorrow and can graciously and wisely offer the hope of the gospel.

In the end, recognizing how our suffering relates to the gospel story allows us to walk victoriously through trials. If we are to find peace and hope *in the midst of* grieving, we must fix our gaze upon our wonderful Savior who loves us with an incomprehensible love. He is the one who will guide us through the fog of despair.

The One Who Makes All the Difference

In his book *Knowing God*, J. I. Packer tells this story:

I walked in the sunshine with a scholar who had effectively forfeited his prospects of academic advancement by clashing with church dignitaries over the gospel of grace. "But it doesn't matter," he said at length, "for I've known God and they haven't." The remark was a mere parenthesis, a passing comment on something I had said, but it has stuck with me and set me thinking.

Not many of us, I think, would ever naturally say that we have known God. The words imply a definiteness and matter-of-factness of experience to which most of us, if we are honest, have to admit that we are still strangers. We claim, perhaps, to have a testimony, and can rattle off our conversion story with the best of them; we say that we *know* God— this after all, is what evangelicals are expected to say; but would it occur to us to say, without hesitation, and with reference to particular events in our personal history that we *have known God*? I doubt it, for I suspect that with most of us experience of God has never become so vivid as that."[1]

I've often thought about this story as the trial of miscarriage has touched my life. From time to time people have marveled at my husband's and my faith as we've confessed the Lord's goodness while walking through such painful events. But it was not our "strong faith" that made this possible. Our confidence in the Lord's lovingkindness is the result of knowing his Word and experiencing his Spirit's comforting presence. It was *knowing God* in these times of pain and suffering that allowed us to come out on the other side with joy and hope for the future. Having *known* him has made all the difference.

This is my desire for this book. If you are currently

experiencing miscarriage or have experienced it in the past, I pray that my imperfect words will be a blessing to your soul, for I endeavor to lead you to the Savior even as you grieve. And if you seek to walk alongside others experiencing this pain, I pray that this book will help you hope in God's sovereignty, and in his grace and goodness toward those who suffer. Whatever your situation, I have the utmost confidence in the Scripture's ability to comfort the weary heart. Therefore, the majority of what I share with you will be taken directly from that precious treasury of wisdom and grace.

* * *

A Prayer for the Suffering Mother

Heavenly Father, I praise you for your goodness in bringing this book into the hands of this suffering sister in Christ. Would you use these chapters to comfort her weary soul and reveal your great love for her? Holy Spirit, would you illuminate your Scriptures to instruct her mind so that she might gain a biblical framework for her suffering? Would you lift the weight of grief that threatens to crush her soul and replace it with your perfect peace? Precious Jesus, would you be ever-present through your Spirit? Lead her, guard her, and uphold her while she walks through the valley of the shadow of death. You are our Great Shepherd, and I trust you to care perfectly for her tender heart.

Though I wish that I could hold her hand and weep great tears of sorrow with her, I know that she has one far greater than me who is holding her close. Divine comforter, be with her now, using the Word to bring her victoriously through this trial, she who has been purchased by the precious blood of Christ. I pray that one day you will grant her the grace necessary to look back upon this horrible time and say with a trembling, awestruck voice, "Even still, I've known God!"

Holy God, I beg you to make yourself and your gospel uniquely beautiful and powerful to this sister in her time of grief. I pray all of this in the powerful name of our Savior, the Lord of Life, Jesus Christ. Amen.

One
AN INHERITANCE OF TEARS

"You just never think something like this will happen to you."

We hear this sort of sentiment all the time in the news, usually spoken through tears by someone who has just experienced tragedy. And yes, the first time a woman views a positive pregnancy test, she rarely assumes she will only have a few short weeks to hold that new life within her. Instead, her mind fills with visions of her precious baby, cradled in her arms. In that moment, miscarriage is usually the furthest thing from a new mother's mind.

When I became pregnant with our first baby, I was elated. I couldn't wait to tell my husband and then share the wonderful news with our family, our friends, and the world! Like most new mothers, I scoured the pages of popular pregnancy books and tried to imagine my precious baby's size and shape with each passing week. Most books, however, included one chapter that I didn't spend much time in: the chapter on miscarriage and stillbirth. In fact, the book that became my "pregnancy bible" *strongly recommended* that I not read that chapter unless it became necessary.[2] After all, no need to worry yourself over something that may not happen.

Until it does.

On that otherwise beautiful spring day when the cramping and bleeding began, the possibility of miscarriage came as a shocking and horrifying revelation to me. When my body went into painful contractions a few days later, my husband and I spent the night in tearful agony. I was left wondering "Why me, God? Why my baby?"

A Valid Question

When terrible things happen for no apparent reason, the most basic question we ask is "Why?" Why does a mudslide wipe out an entire village? Why do parents of young children die of cancer, leaving behind bereaved spouses and bewildered little ones? Why do babies die before they ever have a chance to be held by their mothers and fathers? Why my baby? Why yours?

It will take the rest of this book to even begin to answer that question in a helpful way—a way that does justice to Scripture and the magnificent plan of our sovereign God. But for now, let me just say that in each and every event, whether good or bad, God is always doing more than we could possibly imagine in ways we could never anticipate. His plan to take something altogether awful, like miscarriage, and use it for our good and his glory is beyond our understanding.

Thus, we can never know all the reasons God allows any particular trial to enter our lives. Even the apostle Paul declared, "Oh, the depth of the riches and wisdom and knowledge of God! How unsearchable are his judgments and how inscrutable his ways!" Can you hear Paul worshiping God there in Romans 11:33, giving him glory despite personal uncertainty and maybe even a degree of perplexity? Paul didn't have all the answers; no one ever does. But if you will walk with me through this short book, I believe you can find — through God's Word and the power of his Spirit — a depth of comfort and a tangible joy you may not have believed was even possible.

So let's get started.

The Birth of Death

One thing we can know plainly is why horrible events like miscarriage happen in the first place. When every fiber of our being is crying out, "This is not good! Something about this is terribly wrong!" the Bible doesn't come up empty. In fact, the Bible gives us the only satisfactory explanation for both the existence of such tragedies *and* our natural inclination to grieve them. We needn't look any further than its first few pages, in the book of Genesis, to learn how death and suffering entered our world, and why their very existence strikes us all as inherently wrong.

Genesis 1 describes God's divine act of creation. First, he made the heavens and the earth, as well as light, water, and land. He then filled his creation with vegetation and living things like sea creatures, birds, and animals. After each new addition to his world, he declared it *good*. Nothing was amiss or wrong with anything our holy God formed and put into place. Every bit of it beautifully expressed his own perfection.

Then, this Lord of life completed his creation by placing the first humans, Adam and Eve, into that perfect paradise. He set them above all the rest of the created things as God's unique image-bearers, able to relate to and enjoy communion with their Creator. God commanded them to "be fruitful and multiply and fill the earth and subdue it" (Genesis 1:28). They were God's ambassadors—his regents to the rest of creation. And when God finally finished, he "saw everything that he had made, and behold, it was *very* good" (Genesis 1:31).

We don't really appreciate just *how* good God's creation was until, in Genesis 3, we see what happened when Adam and Eve lost it all. When Eve fell prey to Satan's temptation and convinced her husband to rebel against their Creator, God justly judged their sin with a curse—a curse that affected *everything*.

Because of Adam and Eve's rebellion, God declared that every facet of creation would be forever altered. Eve will now experience extreme pain in childbirth and her relationship to her husband will be permanently warped. Because of Adam's sin, the earth itself will resist his attempts to cultivate it; his work will be difficult and unfulfilling, and ultimately, he (along with the rest of the human race) will die. God had graciously warned Adam in Genesis 2:16–17 that eating from the tree of the knowledge of good and evil would result in his death, and now Adam's disobedience shackled all humanity to that inescapable fate.

Romans 5:12 describes how Adam and Eve's sin ties directly to death, telling us that "sin came into the world through one man [Adam], and death through sin, and so death spread to all men because all sinned." We see here that the only reason death is a part of our lives—the only reason babies do not always grow perfectly within the womb and then go on to grow unhindered outside of it for endless days—is because of sin. The sinfulness we have inherited from our first parents, Adam and Eve, means that we have also inherited their curse: death.

Susannah Spurgeon aptly referred to this as an "inheritance of tears," emphasizing the painful effects of sin that each member of the human race will suffer. She proposed that "tears are the inheritance of earth's children"[3] because, as Romans 3:23 informs us, "*all* have sinned and fall short of the glory of God." Any woman whose womb has been visited by death and has had to say goodbye to her precious baby can readily accept Mrs. Spurgeon's poetic phrasing. Each of us, as descendants of Adam and Eve, are destined to live out our days in a world infected with sin. As a result, we are likely to shed many tears as we await our Savior's final victory over sin and death.

The Infection That Affects Us All

Certainly, the most profound and horrific results of man's rebellion against God were spiritual. Adam and

Eve's choice to disobey God caused every member of the human race to inherit a sin nature, making all of us fully deserving of hell. As descendants of the human race "brought forth in iniquity" (Psalm 51:5), we are "by nature children of wrath" (Ephesians 2:3) and under God's continual judgment. Without Christ's sacrificial death on the cross, our sin separates us from our holy God and makes us his "enemies" (Romans 5:10).

However, as we have already begun to see, much of what was described in the curse was also physical, here-on-this-earth suffering: pain in childbirth, broken relationships, a hostile creation, grueling work, and physical death. These are all descriptions of the world in which Adam and Eve and their children would live out their earthly days.

Following Genesis 3, the Bible goes on to catalog the devastating results of Adam and Eve's rebellion. Generation after generation live (often very difficult lives) and then die, women struggle with barrenness, men kill each other in single acts of rage or during war, governments enslave whole people groups, the poor suffer. I could go on. The point is that what God once declared "good" has become very obviously broken.

The Bible thus describes a life affected in every way by sin. It describes your life and mine. Despite the material prosperity now present in so much of the world, difficulty, conflict, pain, illness, corruption, misunder-standing, and challenges serve as the background noise of our everyday existence. In each of our lives, that noise periodically erupts into a deafening roar as the curse manifests itself in more obvious ways such as disease, disasters, dementia, and death.

Romans 8:18–25 helps us understand how a biological tragedy like death, including miscarriage, fits into the larger scope of the biblical narrative. I will reference this passage often throughout this book, so I will quote it in full here. As you read, pay special attention to what Paul says about the creation (which includes our bodies):

> For I consider that the sufferings of this present time are not worth comparing with the glory that is to be revealed to us. *For the creation waits with eager longing* for the revealing of the sons of God. *For the creation was subjected to futility*, not willingly, but because of him who subjected it, in hope that *the creation itself will be set free from its bondage to corruption* and obtain the freedom of the glory of the children of God. For we know that *the whole creation has been groaning together in the pains of childbirth until now*. And not only the creation, but we ourselves, who have the firstfruits of the Spirit, groan inwardly as we wait eagerly for adoption as sons, *the redemption of our bodies*. For in this hope we were saved. Now hope that is seen is not hope. For who hopes for what he sees? But if we hope for what we do not see, we wait for it with patience. (Romans 8:18–25)

We see from this passage that, as judgment for Adam and Eve's sin, God subjected the *entire* creation to futility.

The choice to rebel against God had permanent, cosmic implications. Since that moment, every single molecule of the universe has been crying out "in the pains of childbirth" for the day when it would be released from its "bondage" to sin. Even our bodies, which are "wasting away" (2 Corinthians 4:16), await their "redemption" through Christ Jesus.

Though Paul mentions "the pains of childbirth" metaphorically here, actual pregnancies are certainly not exempt from the bondage he discusses. Each egg and sperm that unite to form a unique human life are affected by the curse of sin. Wombs, which the Lord created to bring forth new life, no longer function entirely as they ought. They are forever marred by the curse.

In this passage, Paul encourages his readers to place their specific suffering within the wider context of the fall and redemption. He reminds them that the entire world is subjected to futility and must suffer under the curse of sin until the glorious day when God will restore his creation. As we seek to make sense of miscarriage, we must also attempt to recognize and acknowledge it as part of this bigger picture.

Death experienced within the womb is a direct result of sin. While Christ's death on the cross has paid the penalty for our sin once and for all, we still eagerly await the day when our Savior will return and do away with the horrible consequences of sin forever. In this sense, we look forward to his victory over death being fully realized. And all of creation awaits that victory with us! Oh, how we long for his return! In that day our suffering will be eclipsed by the glories of eternal life in Christ Jesus, and our physical bodies will no longer be subjected to decay and brokenness.

Who Sinned, Lord?

If sin is the ultimate cause of miscarriage, women can often wonder if it was their own *personal* sinfulness that caused the death of their child. I'm not referring here to mothers whose sin includes disregarding sound medical advice or behaving recklessly or foolishly during pregnancy. I mean essentially responsible mothers who, struggling under the tragedy of a miscarriage, search their hearts and rack their brains for some spiritual failing that they think could have "caused" it. We may compare ourselves to Christian women who only have successful pregnancies and wonder what's different between us that would produce such horribly different outcomes. When this happens, we have started down a dangerous path— viewing our miscarriage as a reflection of God's feelings toward us.

Does this miscarriage signify God's displeasure in me? Is he punishing me for a lack of faith? Is there something I could have done differently to ensure that God kept my baby alive? Has my sin finally caught up with me?

The answer to all of these questions is a resounding "no." As Christians, God's affections for us are not contingent upon our good performance; they are eternally and irrevocably secured by Jesus' perfect life and substitutionary death.

The problem is that we are prone to gravitate toward a performance-based mentality in our relationship to God, forgetting that the gospel of God's infinite love has been permanently extended to us through the finished work of his Son. We assume that the better we behave, the more God will love us and the less pain and suffering we will experience. How easy it is to miss the fact that this turns God into a cosmic vending machine, dispensing circumstances based on what we "pay." If we have lots of Godward love, lots of faith, and do lots of good works, we get health, wealth, and prosperity. If we don't, God might just allow us to miscarry our babies.

It is exactly this kind of mentality that led the disciples to ask Jesus why a certain man they were passing by had suffered so severely. They looked at their master and said, "Rabbi, who sinned, this man or his parents, that he was born blind?" They assumed that his lack of sight was a direct result of *personal* sin—either his or his parents. In his response, the Lord turns our natural expectations upside down. "Jesus answered, 'It was not that this man sinned, or his parents, *but that the works of God might be displayed in him*'" (John 9:3).

We have no reason to believe that this blind man had faith in Jesus. If he did not, he was still God's enemy, and fully deserving of any suffering that might come his way.[4] And this makes Jesus' response even more amazing. Given the perfect opportunity to draw a connection between personal sin and specific hardship, Jesus turned it down. If he wanted us to think in those terms, this would have been an obvious time to say so. Yet on that particular matter he chose not only to be deafeningly silent, but to point us in a completely different direction.

Here in John 9:3, Jesus is telling us that each and every trial we face has a divine design. Trials are inevitable for broken people who live in a broken world. But what we must remember during suffering is that our sovereign God has orchestrated our hardships *to accomplish something*. (In the case of the blind man, he wanted to show Jesus' miraculous healing abilities and prove his divinity.) And while it is equally true that our hardships are ultimately meant to bring glory to Christ, as God's beloved children, we can always rest in the comforting knowledge that our God means our trials for our good (Romans 8:28), a concept that we will explore further in coming chapters.

Although I understand the tendency to see miscarriage as punishment, I also believe that such thinking is horribly misguided. It not only tosses out the reality that through Jesus' sacrifice on the cross, our sins are forgiven, but it replaces that glorious truth with a Christless universe ruled by self-righteousness and karma. As children of God who have been forgiven of our sins through the blood of Christ, let us instead be vigilant to remind ourselves of our right standing before God.

Romans 8:1 says, "There is therefore now no condemnation for those who are in Christ Jesus." This means that if you have placed your faith in the substitutionary death of Christ on the cross for your sins, then each of those sins—past, present, and future—has already been paid for. The eternal Son of God became a man and tasted the sting of death, so that we could be delivered from it (Hebrews 2:9)! Women who have miscarried need not fear that God has chosen to punish them by taking their baby's life. He has already punished his Son. We who have been bought with the precious blood of Christ are no longer enemies of God but beloved children whom he loves with the undying, unwavering affection of a father. (If you have never trusted in Jesus or for some other reason find yourself reading this under the heavy burden of your own grief, please cast that burden upon him. The Son of God lived and died and rose again so that you could live — really live, even right now — in him.) We need no longer exist as children of wrath, but as recipients of his love, grace, and mercy (Ephesians 2:3–7).

A Note to the Friends of Sufferers

Job lost his farm, his servants, his children, and his health. His friends thought it was surely his own fault. They brought up areas of his life where he *must* have been lacking in obedience to God. What they were not aware of was that God had *allowed* Satan to afflict Job in order to *prove* his faithfulness to God. It was not Job's sinfulness that brought about his suffering, but his righteousness! God's purpose in Job's afflictions was not to punish Job, but to display God's glory to Satan, Job, Job's friends, and ultimately to every person who would ever read Job's story in Scripture. But neither Job nor his friends were aware of this, so his friends offered the only explanation they could conceive of: that Job's sin was to blame.

D. A. Carson has this sharp warning for those tempted to equate suffering with failures of personal holiness:

> Most emphatically, this does not mean that every bit of suffering is the immediate consequence of a particular sin. That is a hideous piece of heresy, capable of inflicting untold mental anguish. It would mean that people who suffer the most in this world must be those who have sinned the most in this world; and that is demonstrably untrue, both in the Bible and in experience....
>
> Indeed, one of the functions of biblical teaching about rewards in heaven and degrees of punishment in hell...is that it explains in part why there is no equitable distribution of punishments here. Some answers we are not going to receive here; we shall have to wait for the Lord's return before justice is completely done, and seen to be done.[5]

Sufferers often have friends like Job's. When a woman miscarries, they hope to provide some kind of relief to her anguish, with the best of intentions, by grasping at any explanation they can. They may point to spiritual weaknesses that God could be seeking to rid her of, or they may rush to point out the good things God surely has in store for her future. Yes, there will come a time for self-introspection and growth in holiness as a result of every miscarriage, but those who desire to comfort the grieving would do well to heed the admonition to simply grieve with those who grieve, and weep with those who weep (Romans 12:15).

What to Expect from a Sin-Broken World

For many of us, the effects of this fallen world seem like distant theological concepts that carry little weight in everyday life. As a result, we live with expectations befitting a pre-fall Eden, rather than a sin-broken Earth. We *expect* to live healthy, fulfilled lives. We *expect* to have marriages in which we perfectly understand and communicate with our spouses. We *expect* to become pregnant easily, carry our babies full-term, and deliver them in perfect health. Our hearts yearn for the creation to function as God intended it to, and thus we don't naturally *expect* pain, discord, or death. Yet, this is exactly the inescapable inheritance we've received from our first parents.

The daily manifestations of God's beautiful grace, which we are blessed to experience despite our fallen state, are like windows into a world we do not yet fully inhabit—a world where God's goodness flows, unhindered by sin, to his created beings. A world with no more pain or suffering or death. In short: heaven.

Yet we tend to believe that we deserve such comforts and perfections in *this* world. We picture ourselves living out our lives in peaceful delight, doing work we always love, serving in churches where nothing ever goes seriously wrong. We buy pregnancy books, fully expecting our babies to grow according to each chapter's description. Rarely do we consider the awful truth that our babies are conceived in sin-infected bodies walking around in a sin-infected world. Indeed, even our babies' genetic make-up is subjected to the same futility as the rest of creation. Though pregnancy books may encourage us to put off distressing thoughts such as miscarriage and stillbirth, a biblical worldview *demands* that we have a realistic view of what pregnancy can and sometimes does look like in a post-fall world.

It certainly isn't my aim to paint a hopeless picture for those already experiencing grief. There is real, good, credible hope in the gospel of Jesus Christ for every daughter of Eve. I want to encourage you — if possible — with the knowledge that miscarriage is indeed a *terrible* thing. Women who experience miscarriage rightly feel as though something horrific just happened to them and their child. They need not feel obligated to treat the event as something common that they should simply "get over" and "move on" from. It *is* common, but that does not lessen its horror! Miscarriage, like every other manifestation of the fall, is the opposite of what God intended for our world — it is not good, it is *very* bad. Knowing this is essential to our finding encouragement in Christ.

For many women, miscarriage will be one of their first experiences with the serious physical effects of the fall. I distinctly remember the emotions that surged through me when we lost our first baby to miscarriage. Suddenly, the idea of death took on a whole new meaning. As my womb was robbed of the life it once carried, the groaning of creation became terribly personal. Later on, when I delivered the lifeless body of another of our precious babies who had died at 15 weeks gestation, my soul yearned like never before for Christ to return and do away with death forever.

Eyes That Glisten

Before Jesus raised his friend Lazarus from the dead, we are told that he was "deeply moved" by the situation before him. As he spoke with Lazarus' grieving sisters and took in the scene of mourners, the horrid consequences of sin were set starkly before him. What we often miss in this passage is that the phrase "deeply moved" actually carries less a sense of sadness than it does a sense of indignation.[6] Jesus was angry that death had come to Lazarus' house and angry that his friends were experiencing its pain. Our God wept not only out of sorrow, but also out of righteous anger as he came face to face with the enemy he had come to defeat.

In fact, the Bible literally refers to death as Jesus' "last enemy" (1 Corinthians 15:26). It is the foe that he will one day completely banish when he restores his kingdom on Earth. In that day, "he will wipe away every tear from [our] eyes, and death shall be no more, neither shall there be mourning, nor crying, nor pain anymore, for the former things have passed away" (Revelation 21:4). This is the glorious hope set before us. Though we currently live in a world infected with sin, and therefore with death, a day is coming when sin and death will be no more and every tear will be gently wiped away by our loving Savior, Jesus Christ. He who loved us to the point of death—even death on a cross—will minister to our wounded hearts. His perfect love will overshadow any suffering we have encountered on this earth. It is for this reason that Paul was able to say that we do not grieve as those who have no hope (1 Thessalonians 4:13). Undoubtedly we grieve, but we do so as those who know we will one day be raised from the dead to a new life with our Savior! We grieve, but as those who know that grieving itself will one day come to an end.

I began this chapter with Susannah Spurgeon's eloquent quote, "Tears are the inheritance of earth's children." As Romans 8 reminded us, we are not alone in our suffering. Death is a part of everyone's life experience. Some mothers have lost their babies, others have lost their toddlers, still others, their teenagers. And so on. Unless the Lord returns, every one of us will one day find out that we ourselves are dying and must say goodbye to those we love. All of earth's children must suffer and experience death, but not without hope. So I take courage from the way Mrs. Spurgeon ended the devotional from which I quoted earlier: "Tears may, and must come; but if they gather in eyes that are constantly *looking up* to [God] and heaven, they will glisten with the brightness of the coming glory."[7]

The eyes of those who have miscarried are easily filled with tears. The pain of losing a baby is often too much to bear, but this world is not as it was meant to be, and it is not what it will be. We must look up to our Savior and entrust our hearts to the one who has tasted death for us and has promised to do away with it forever.

Let our eyes glisten with the coming glory of the Son of God—our mighty Conqueror and loving Savior.

*   *   *

A Prayer for the Suffering Mother

Father, please comfort this dear sister with the knowledge that she is not alone in her suffering. What she has experienced is a painful manifestation of the curse of which we all partake. Remind her that it is for this very reason that you sent your eternal Son to live a sinless life, to die a sinner's death, and to be resurrected from the grave. If she has not truly embraced this truth for herself, may this experience of personal loss drive her to the cross where she can find forgiveness for her sins and hope for her eternal soul! If she is a sister in Christ who has placed her trust in your substitutionary work on the cross, would you help her treasure that work all the more dearly? You hate death and suffering infinitely more than she ever could, and you came to make propitiation for sin, so that one day these foes would be no more. We look forward to your coming, Lord; we long for your final victory. It's in the victorious name of Jesus that I ask these things. Amen.

Two
THE GOOD BUT DIFFICULT PLANS OF GOD

Shortly after we miscarried our first baby, we returned to our church to worship alongside our brothers and sisters in Christ. At the time, we were members of a congregation near the seminary my husband was attending. This congregation was filled with young families and seemed to be in a continual state of baby production. At every meeting, car-seat carriers lined the aisles and pregnant bellies protruded from nearly every pew.

That Sunday morning, as I looked around at my pregnant sisters in Christ, my eyes filled with tears. How desperately I wanted what they had, and how difficult it was to accept that God had chosen otherwise for me. In that moment, as in so many thereafter, I had to make a conscious decision to preach God's good sovereignty to my heart. I prayed that the Holy Spirit would conform my heart to his Word, transforming my emotions

from overwhelming grief to peaceful trust. Through
his enabling grace, I chose to cry out with the psalmist,
"Satisfy [me] in the morning with your steadfast love, that
[I] may rejoice and be glad all [my] days" (Psalm 90:14),
even though it didn't feel as though God was loving me
or that there was anything to rejoice in.

Who's in Control?

Women who've experienced miscarriage have asked me
if there was any point in praying for the safety of their
unborn babies if God was ultimately going to allow
them to die. These women feel defeated and betrayed
by the Lord. But packed into this one question are many
other questions about God's sovereignty over events that
unfold within the womb. Does God really do all that he
wants to do? Does God hear our prayers? And if so, do
they make a difference? Is death stronger than God?

As I've filtered all this through the biblical doctrine
of God's sovereignty, I'm left with one paradoxical
conclusion: the reason it makes sense to pray for our
unborn babies, even those we will eventually miscarry, is
precisely because God is in control of their lives. For if
he were not ultimately sovereign over all that happens
in our wombs, he would not be God at all. Prayer itself
would be useless if God did not have the ability to act in
response to it.

But the sovereignty of God is not the only divine
attribute on trial in these questions. When we discuss
God's sovereignty, we must also consider the goodness
of his character. Let's face it, we tend to think that we

know what's best for our lives. When God doesn't deliver according to our preferences, we question his wisdom and love. We treat God like a magical genie who's obligated to answer our prayers in a way that pleases *us*. In reality, however, we are talking about the holy God of the universe, whose goodness, loving-kindness, and wisdom infinitely surpass our greatest imaginings.

Though his sovereign *ability* to answer our prayers demands that we ask for the godly desires of our heart, it is his infinite *goodness* that demands we trust him when he doesn't fulfill those desires.

Sovereignty: A Single Hair and a Billion Stars

In the previous chapter, we saw that death is a result of the fall of Adam and Eve; that evil, horrible events like miscarriage are a part of the curse; and that each of us partake in this curse as Adam's descendants. However, the Bible does not support the idea that God is surprised when bad things happen in his world. In fact, the Bible teaches the opposite. Our holy God not only knows each and every event that will occur in our lives before it happens, he actually plans our lives down to the smallest detail—again, for our good and his glory.

It may seem like a disturbing proposition to say that God plans miscarriages. How could God desire for anyone to go through such terrible suffering? Why would he allow a baby's life to end if he could have preserved it? These are difficult questions that we must

wrestle with. Many times, in an effort to conform God
to our own image apart from the light of his Word, we
decide he couldn't possibly be in control—or that it
would be better if he weren't. But would it? Would it be
better if God was unable to accomplish his will or didn't
know every detail about the future? If we are honest
with ourselves, we must confess that both proposi-
tions—God being in control and God not being in
control—have challenging implications for our human
understanding. But we must be willing to admit that our
abilities to reason and understand the infinite God are
extremely limited. And if we, as Christians, accept that
God has given us his Word to teach us things about him
that we could never otherwise know, then we must turn
to Scripture for answers.

Consider God's sovereignty in general. How does
the Bible describe God in relationship to his creation? Is
he merely an observer or does he orchestrate events?

In speaking about Jesus, Hebrews 1:3 tells us that
"he is the radiance of the glory of God and the exact
imprint of his nature, and he upholds the universe by the
word of his power." Here we see that the power of Jesus'
word holds together the entire universe—that is, all of
creation. To put it another way, what Jesus decides will
happen with the sun, moon, and stars happens; what he
says will happen with our bodies and with our babies,
happens—nothing is outside of his dominion. Colos-
sians 1:17 echoes the same thought when it says, "in
him all things hold together." Every molecule in our
bodies and in our children's bodies is held together by

our Savior, and nothing occurs without his permission. Indeed, the Bible presents God not as a casual observer but as the sustainer and orchestrator of all things. From the flip of a coin (Proverbs 16:33) to the decisions of kings (Proverbs 21:1), God works "all things according to the counsel of his will" (Ephesians 1:11).

Jesus encouraged his disciples with this truth about the Father's sovereign control, knowing that they would encounter persecution and trials as they set out to proclaim the gospel. No matter what happens, we can rest in our God: "Are not two sparrows sold for a penny? And not one of them will fall to the ground apart from your Father. But even the hairs of your head are all numbered. Fear not, therefore; you are of more value than many sparrows" (Matthew 10:29–31).

If our great God controls the life span of a small bird and knows when a single hair falls from our head, is he not also in control of our lives, which are much more valuable to him? Are not babies within the womb, who are created in the image of God, more valuable to him than a bird in our backyard or a hair swept up in our bathrooms? Of course they are! For this reason, we can be certain that no harm will come to them outside of his loving will.

Little Lives Lost

But harm *has* come to them, hasn't it? It can be especially difficult to reconcile God's sovereignty with the terrible pain of losing a child. An aging adult, perhaps, but a baby? A son or daughter who will never be held, kissed, or embraced? This seems unreasonable. Surely God did not plan for these little lives to end so quickly. Surely he is just as frustrated by their untimely deaths as we are. And this is a perfectly reasonable thought process—apart from the revealed Word of God.

We have seen that death is an unnatural result of sin's infestation. We have recounted how Jesus wept with indignation over the death of Lazarus. And we know that the last enemy he will defeat is death itself. So we can know beyond question that the death of our babies grieves the Lord of life. Yet we must simultaneously embrace the truth that he is sovereign over each of our life spans—even the shortest of them. Let us look at a familiar passage of Scripture and apply it to the babies we've lost to miscarriage:

> For you formed my inward parts;
>> you knitted me together in my mother's womb.
> I praise you, for I am fearfully and wonderfully made.
> Wonderful are your works;
>> my soul knows it very well.
> My frame was not hidden from you,
> when I was being made in secret,
>> intricately woven in the depths of the earth.
> Your eyes saw my unformed substance;
> in your book were written, every one of them,
>> the days that were formed for me,
>> when as yet there was none of them. (Psalm 139:13–16)

Usually we reference this passage to celebrate life and prove the unique personhood of each baby growing within the womb. We marvel at the way God fashions each of us with his loving hand. Rarely, however, do we also consider that according to this passage, the days God has decreed for a life may be few rather than many; rarely do we think that he may allow a baby to grow only for a few weeks before his or her life is complete. And yet, from this passage we can say with confidence that God not only creates each baby, he also numbers each of their days — just as he does for each of us. He may have planned a long 80 years for you or a short 45 years for me, but for babies lost to miscarriage, he has planned mere weeks.

The curse manifests itself in each of our lives through physical death, but as Job so eloquently put it, it is God who appoints the limits that we cannot pass (Job 14:5). It is God who plans each lost pregnancy, from the moment of conception to the moment the child is taken. We must cry out for ourselves and for each of our children, "O Lord, make me know my end and what is the measure of my days; let me know how fleeting I am!" (Psalm 39:4). Whether we have experienced the pain of miscarriage, or whether we simply fear that experience, we must ask the Lord to show us how fleeting the life of each person is — even the lives of our unborn children.

Can I Really Trust Him?

Matt Redman's song "Blessed Be Your Name" often ran through my mind after each of my miscarriages. Its tempo is so upbeat that when it was sung at church, I couldn't even bring myself to sing along without sobs bursting from my mouth. I usually had to sing it in the quietness of my heart as the tears ran down my cheeks. The words I could once sing so easily were now filled with weight, experience, and pain. Sweet words had become hard words.

The song moves through various seasons of life, good and bad, each time emphasizing that the Lord's name is to be praised no matter what the circumstances. Verses like this one were especially touching to me after my miscarriages:

> Blessed be your name
> On the road marked with suffering
> Though there's pain in the offering
> Blessed be Your name.[8]

Never before had I experienced so much pain as I sought to worship my God. In those sweet moments of worship, I fought to accept his sovereign will for myself and my babies. There was certainly great pain in the offering! Perhaps even more challenging, however, was the refrain which repeats, "You give and take away, you give and take away, my heart will choose to say, Lord blessed be Your name!" Though I could rarely bring myself to sing these words aloud, my soul was thankful for the biblical counsel it received through them.

This song references Job's own bold and courageous proclamation after learning that he had lost his wealth, servants, and children all in one horrific day. Through seemingly freak accidents, random forces of nature, and arbitrary thefts, Job had lost everything—yet he firmly believed that it was God himself who had orchestrated the terrible events of that day.

Just paragraphs before Job's trials begin, we are given a backstage pass, an opportunity to witness secret happenings before God's throne. We see that God *allowed* Satan to afflict Job in order to prove his blamelessness. Job, however, doesn't know this. He is left to see his trials play out in the same way we see ours play out: moment by moment, with no explanation or specific cosmic backstory.

Job's baffling response to his horrific suffering vindicates the confidence God had in him. When Job's whole world came crashing down around his head in a single day, Job responded, "Naked I came from my mother's womb, and naked shall I return. The LORD gave, and the LORD has taken away; blessed be the name of the LORD" (Job 1:21).

This response seems illogical. Suffering extreme loss, Job not only has the audacity to claim that God sovereignly orchestrated the unfolding events, but also that God remains worthy of praise through it all.

How do we become more like Job? How do we go from agreeing with the abstract truth of God's sovereignty to genuinely praising his goodness amid wrenching personal loss? How do we acknowledge that it was *God* who first gave and then so quickly took away these precious lives? How do we bless God's name along with Job? Operating from a worldly perspective, we would turn our backs on God altogether. After all, it was *he* who gave and then took away! There's no denying this, so at the human level nothing could be more natural than to curse God's name in the face of such painful loss. In fact, that's exactly what Job's wife recommends that he do.

Cursing God amid tragedy is natural...unless we *know him*. That's the key. For if we know God as our Father who is ever good and wise and loving, we can trust him, truly and deeply, even in the most difficult of circumstances.

Goodness: Seeing God as He Is

In order to trust God when his will is difficult to accept, we must know who he is. To rest in his difficult providences, we must have confidence in his character. We must know that he is indeed trustworthy; we must know that he is good. But what does that mean?

God's *goodness* is the culmination of his justice, love, wisdom, kindness, and purity. In all these things—and in every other facet of his character—God is altogether good and worthy of praise.

As we might expect, the Bible is replete with expressions of God's goodness, and the psalms alone provide plenty of examples. Psalm 119:68 says that God *is* good and *does* good. Psalm 34:8 encourages us to "taste and see" the Lord's goodness and to take "refuge in him." Psalm 106:1 proclaims, "Oh give thanks to the LORD, for he is good, for his steadfast love endures forever!" The psalmists believe that God's goodness motivates his good works toward his people (see Psalm 145 as an example). God's expressions of love and compassion toward humanity prove his inherent, perfect, and unchanging goodness. They testify to the fact that "God is light, and in him is no darkness at all" (1 John 1:5).

What we must struggle to understand, of course, is how his goodness can also be expressed through the suffering he allows to enter our lives. When the world is not "all as it should be," how can we still bless God's name as good? Romans 8:28 tells us that "for those who love God all things work together for good, for those who are called according to his purpose." Therefore, we must assume that even something as horrible as miscarriage can be considered good as it passes through the Lord's sovereign hand for his good purposes. Though the trial itself is altogether bad (and only exists because of sin), the purposes of God are always good and wise.

When Nothing Seems Right, It Might Just Be Perfect

Let's look at a story from the Old Testament that illustrates this tension between the consequences of evil and how God uses it for good. You may be familiar with Joseph and his coat of many colors, but many Sunday school lessons miss the fact that the story has far more to do with God's good sovereignty than with an interesting garment. Joseph, the great-grandson of Abraham, is the central character in a chain of unfortunate events—all of them planned by God and all of them with a vital and wonderful purpose.

At age 17, Joseph was sold into slavery by his own jealous brothers. Once a favored son in God's chosen family, Joseph suddenly found himself a powerless slave in a distant land with an alien culture. But God's sovereign hand did not depart from Joseph for a moment. In the Lord's providence, Joseph was sold to Potiphar, an influential officer of Pharaoh. Of course, that encouraging development soon took a turn for the worse when Potiphar's wife attempted to seduce him. When Joseph refused her, she falsely accused *him* of making advances. Outraged, her husband threw the innocent Joseph into prison.

Any reasonable onlooker would have seen this as an unqualified disaster. Yet as the story continues, we are told that "the LORD was with Joseph and showed him steadfast love" (Genesis 39:21). In fact, that jail was exactly where God wanted Joseph to be. It was there that God allowed Joseph to interpret the dreams of two fellow inmates, which ultimately allowed him the extraordinary opportunity to interpret the dreams of Pharaoh. Those dreams revealed that Egypt would soon experience a severe famine, and Pharaoh put Joseph in charge of preparations. Thus was Egypt saved along with neighboring peoples, including Joseph's brothers. Incredibly, it was through the horrible events the Lord allowed in Joseph's life—enslavement and wrongful imprisonment—that Joseph could provide food for his own estranged family. Through mysterious providence, the Lord preserved his chosen people and continued the genealogical line of the Savior.

Joseph himself made this startling connection when he confronted his traitorous brothers: "God sent me before you to preserve for you a remnant on earth, and to keep alive for you many survivors" (Genesis 45:7). Later, after his entire family settled in the land of Egypt, he again assured his brothers, "As for you, you meant evil against me, but *God meant it for good*, to bring it about that many people should be kept alive, as they are today" (Genesis 50:20). Does this mean that Joseph's brothers had not sinned? No, their actions were certainly wrong. But through the extreme ups and downs of his life, Joseph could see the good and sovereign hand of his God.

Two important themes are expressed through Joseph's story. First, God sovereignly controls the events in each of our lives. Second, we may not always understand God's reasons, but we can trust that they are always *good*.

Remember His Love

Trusting God's character when you cannot understand his purposes is pivotal to accepting a difficult providence like miscarriage. For this reason, I would like to invite you to "taste and see that the LORD *is* good" (Psalm 34:8) by contemplating with me the incomprehensible love with which he has loved you in Christ Jesus.

In chapter one, we spent some time looking at Romans 8, where Paul explained that God subjected all of creation to futility as a consequence of Adam and Eve's sin. But this curse was not our good God's ultimate goal. Instead, what he had in mind was the certain hope of future freedom, "hope that the creation itself will be set free from its bondage to corruption and obtain the freedom of the glory of the children of God" (Romans 8:20–21).

How would God do this? It has always been his plan to crush Satan through the seed of the woman (Genesis 3 foretold this). Though sin entered the world through Adam, righteousness and forgiveness have entered the world through Jesus Christ (Romans 5:17).

It is therefore God's sovereign goodness that Jesus was "delivered up according to the *definite plan* and *foreknowledge of God*" (Acts 2:23). Even though sinful men with sinful motives nailed our sinless Savior to the cross, God alone orchestrated every moment of the crucifixion. Why? Because of love. John 3:16 says, "For God so loved the world, that he gave his only Son, that whoever believes in him should not perish but have eternal life." The Father willingly sacrificed his beloved Son on our behalf so he might forgive our sins and reconcile us to him. Because of love, the Father made a way for sinners to experience eternal life rather than death.

We must let this ultimate expression of God's good sovereignty fill our hearts with peace. Only then can we face the unquestionably difficult trial of miscarriage. Note how Paul follows that passage on suffering in Romans 8 with reassuring words: "If God is for us, who can be against us? He who did not spare his own Son but gave him up for us all, how will he not also with him give us all things?" (Romans 8:31–32). We must choose to believe (because it is true!) that the one who went to such great lengths to prove his love for us has not made a mistake in allowing us to miscarry. Our good and loving God did not spare his Son but gave him up for us, and this same God sovereignly orchestrated the loss of our babies; we can therefore humbly trust that his painful providence is *meant for* and *will produce* our ultimate good.

* * *

A Prayer for the Suffering Mother

Sovereign Lord, what a comfort to know that you are in control of all things! Even in this tragedy, we can have confidence that your wisdom and goodness are at work. I pray that you would fill this sister in Christ with a peaceful trust in your great love for her, and that the knowledge of your love would comfort her as she mourns the loss of her precious baby. We know that you do not allow harm to come to your children without good reason, so I ask that you would help her by the power of your Holy Spirit to trust you in this difficult providence. When she questions your wisdom, would you draw her close to your heart and allow her to remember the cross, where you bled and died for her sins, so that she could have eternal life? It is in the name of our good and sovereign Savior, Jesus Christ, that I pray. Amen.

Three
OUR GOOD SHEPHERD

I awoke from the anesthesia into a different world. The last remnants of my pregnancy — and my baby — had been removed from my body by a surgeon's skillful hand. The bright future I had envisioned for our family had been replaced by a painful reality. Life had been exchanged for death, and the womb where my baby once grew was now empty. I had known beforehand that my baby was gone, for I had delivered most of the pregnancy in our apartment. Still, this final step put a painful last seal on a horrific chapter of my life. I rode home with my husband and mother oblivious to anything but my deep feelings of loss.

Loss Invisible

Few people understand the pain a woman feels when she learns that her unborn baby has died. The depth of her suffering is understandably intense, but because of the hidden nature of her loss, few people can relate to her grief. In reality, her suffering may go completely unnoticed. After all, most miscarriages occur before a pregnancy is obvious, an invisibility that only multiplies the grieving mother's pain.

If she shares the tragedy of the miscarriage with family and friends, they often don't know how to respond helpfully. How do they mourn a life they never experienced and may not even have known about? Even a caring and sensitive husband can find it difficult to understand the intense grief his wife may experience. The mother, on the other hand, has felt the physical effects of her pregnancy and perhaps watched the child's tiny movements on an ultrasound. It's possible that she even felt the first miraculous flutters of her baby kicking! Her child may have dominated her thoughts and prayers, making the loss tangible and severely painful. When others forget—often quite quickly—about the life she once carried, her grief only grows heavier.

For a woman in this situation, spending time with other mothers of childbearing age can be particularly difficult. Offhand remarks that would seem innocent enough in another context can feel like a twisting of the knife: "Oh, you'll understand when *you're* a mother," or, "I can't wait until this pregnancy is over! This baby is killing me!" People who say things like this rarely intend to cause a mourning mother further pain, but she will feel their sting keenly. After all, she would gladly accept the physical difficulties of pregnancy if it meant having her baby back; she longs to be a mother once more. Comments like these leave her feeling isolated, misunderstood, and alone in her grief.

God Knows and Understands

As I write this chapter, my dear sister-in-law is experiencing the pain of miscarriage. It was her first pregnancy, full of promise and hope. Only a few days ago, we celebrated with her and her husband as they announced the new life blossoming within her womb. Now, like so many other women before her, she mourns the death of her baby. How desperately I wish that I lived closer and could hold her in my arms as she weeps for her unborn child. How I wish that I could comfort her in person, as someone who has also suffered miscarriage, rather than over the phone or through text messages.

However, the comfort I could offer pales in comparison to what the gospel can accomplish for her. I offer specific empathy and understanding, but Jesus, our loving Savior, is the most gracious and tender comforter. If we could only understand the depth of his love for each member of his blood-bought church, we would never fail to come to him in our times of greatest desperation! He and he alone knows us intimately, understands our suffering perfectly, and comforts us effectively. Such was the encouragement of Joseph Scriven in his beloved hymn:

> What a Friend we have in Jesus, all our sins and griefs to bear!
> What a privilege to carry everything to God in prayer!
> O what peace we often forfeit, O what needless pain we bear,

All because we do not carry everything to God in prayer.

Have we trials and temptations? Is there trouble anywhere?
We should never be discouraged; take it to the Lord in prayer.
Can we find a friend so faithful who will all our sorrows share?
Jesus knows our every weakness; take it to the Lord in prayer.

Are we weak and heavy laden, cumbered with a load of care?
Precious Savior, still our refuge, take it to the Lord in prayer.
Do your friends despise, forsake you? Take it to the Lord in prayer!
In His arms He'll take and shield you; you will find a solace there.

Blessed Savior, Thou hast promised Thou wilt all our burdens bear.
May we ever, Lord, be bringing all to Thee in earnest prayer.
Soon in glory bright unclouded there will be no need for prayer;
Rapture, praise, and endless worship will be our sweet portion there.

Women who miscarry often feel isolated in their grief because of the intensely personal loss they've experienced. They must remember, or perhaps discover for the first time, that their Savior is ready and willing to comfort them in their sorrow. Indeed, even the feelings of isolation can be a great blessing, for isolation from all worldly comforts forces us to draw comfort from the Lord himself.

In his anguish, the psalmist David said that God counted his tossings and kept his tears (Psalm 56:8). That is, he believed that God intimately understood his personal grief. We can have the same confidence that God sees our suffering and knows how deeply we mourn. Nothing goes unnoticed: he knows our own hearts and minds even better than we do (1 Chronicles 28:9). He sees our pain, he hears our cries, and he is perfectly suited to help us in our time of need.

No Stranger to Suffering

At the heart of the Bible is the gospel, and at the heart of the gospel is the unswerving, undeserved, and incomprehensible love of God for his people. Since the fall of Adam and Eve, humanity's history has been characterized by pain and suffering. Blood flows through the storyline of our Bibles as predominately as the ink they are printed with. Just as God decreed, sinful mankind lives under a curse of pain, toil, and death from one generation to the next. Indeed, the apostle Paul tells us that death *reigned* through Adam and his offspring until Christ came (Romans 5:17). Since that fateful day in the garden when Adam and Eve chose to rebel, the human race has been subjected to the rule of sin and misery.

But our loving God sent his eternal Son to deliver us from the shackles of pain and death. Jesus came to rescue his beloved people from the eternal judgment they deserved for their sin. He did this not by triumphantly bursting into our world with the power and majesty his eternal holiness would suggest, but by humbly taking on the frailty of human flesh and willingly entering into humanity's suffering. In a startling display of love, the holy God of the universe chose to be conceived within the weak and vulnerable womb of a virgin and develop there for nine months before being born into our sin-soaked world. He then lived an ordinary (though sinless!) and pain-filled life amongst his finite creatures. He felt the frailty of the human body, saw the pain of death all around him, and experienced the ongoing temptation toward sin all the days of his earthly life (Hebrews 4:15).

Jesus entered our world and partook of the inheritance *we* had secured through sin, so that one day we could partake of the glorious inheritance he would secure *for us* through his sacrificial death on the cross (1 Peter 1:3–4). He did this to defeat humanity's ancient enemies, sin and death. God promised this very solution to Adam and Eve after they rebelled: though Eve would suffer the curse of painful and difficult childbearing (something starkly illustrated in miscarriage), it would be *through* childbearing that the rescuer would come. It would be through Adam and Eve's offspring that Satan, and his reign of death, would finally be defeated (Genesis 3:15).

But before this happened, the "offspring" would suffer personal sacrifice; God decreed that the serpent (Satan) would bruise the offspring's heel (Genesis 3:15). In other words, the way of Jesus' victory would be paved by misery as he entered into man's cursed condition, making him a worthy substitute for his fallen people (Isaiah 53:4).

> Man of Sorrows! what a name
> For the Son of God, who came
> Ruined sinners to reclaim.
> Hallelujah! What a Savior![9]

And so, on that spectacular night more than 2,000 years ago, the God of the universe took on human flesh. He was born into our world through blood and water as a tiny, helpless baby. He was a heavenly king, but his people didn't recognize him as such. Indeed, he had come to rescue them from the very sin that prevented them from doing so.

The incarnation offers beautiful hope for the woman who has miscarried. The death of a baby within the womb is a painful reminder—if not one of the most fundamental expressions—of death's curse over humanity. The good news is that Jesus came to reverse exactly that curse. Mankind was created to multiply and to fill the earth, subduing and caring for it as God's regents, but humanity struggles to fulfill this basic function. Husbands and wives groan under this devastating reality as they watch their precious offspring die even before they are born. Many of our children return to the dust before we do, forcing us to observe helplessly the tragic wages of sin.

The Savior was born into this broken reality. Our God chose to enter our world through flesh and blood, entering *our suffering* in order to free us from it. The eternal Son of God became a Son of Man, first by becoming a zygote, and then an embryo, and then a fetus. Finally, he was victoriously born into our world as a fully developed baby. This was necessary so that he could wage war against the very foe that has taken so many precious, pre-born babies:

> Since therefore the children share in flesh and blood, [Jesus] himself likewise partook of the same things, that through death he might destroy the one who has the power of death, that is, the devil, and deliver all those who through fear of death were subject to lifelong slavery" (Hebrews 2:14–15).

> O loving wisdom of our God,
> When all was sin and shame
> A second Adam to the fight
> And to the rescue came.

> O wisest love, that flesh and blood
> That did in Adam fail
> Should strive afresh against the foe
> Should strive and should prevail.[10]

Tears of Blood

Entering into humanity's suffering allowed our holy
God to experience the effects of sin as we do. He doesn't
only see our pain from a distance, and he doesn't only
collect our tears in his bottle as a faithful observer. Rather,
he himself has shed tears of pain and sorrow—tears of
unhindered grief (John 11:35, Hebrews 5:7, Matthew
27:46). *His* precious tears are now counted among the
waves of grief experienced by the human race throughout time. We are told in Hebrews 2:17–18 that Jesus
endured suffering and temptation so that he could be
a merciful and faithful high priest able to help us in
our times of weakness. Doesn't every woman who has
miscarried long for someone to perfectly understand her
pain? According to Paul, Jesus can and does comfort all
those who share in his suffering (2 Corinthians 1:5).

In the 33 years that Jesus walked this dusty earth, he
was subjected to all of the same temptations and trials
that we are. His sufferings allow him to identify with his
suffering people in many ways, but I want to focus on three
specific ways in which Jesus can relate to—and therefore
perfectly comfort—the woman who has miscarried. It is
my prayer that the pain women have experienced in miscarriage will allow them to see Jesus' *voluntary*, sacrificial
suffering with new intensity and gratitude. As we look at
these three ways in which Jesus has suffered, may it remind
us of his willingness and ability to comfort us during our
times of grief. May it increase our love and affection for our
marvelous God! For he truly is the "good shepherd [who]
lays down his life for his sheep" (John 10:11).

Loneliness and Isolation

The trial of miscarriage is unique. Those who have not experienced the pregnancy may find it hard to understand, so the bereaved mother often carries the unseen loss quietly within her heart, leaving her feeling alone. But there is one perfectly suited to sympathize with her pain and feelings of loneliness. When tempted to feel isolated and misunderstood, she must run to Jesus. Though deserving of honor and praise and adoration, Jesus was "despised and rejected by men" (Isaiah 53:3). He never felt at home in this world, saying "foxes have holes, and birds of the air have nests, but the Son of Man has nowhere to lay his head" (Luke 9:58). The Savior's life was often characterized by loneliness, injustice, and misunderstanding.

As the perfect substitute for his people, it was essential that Jesus live victoriously in ways that fallen humanity could not. But in many respects, this led to isolation. Consider how Jesus, amid great spiritual torment the night before his murder, asked his closest friends simply to stay awake and pray with him. Of course they could not. He would soon face the greatest trial a man has ever suffered, but not even his friends could understand his agony. How could they? They were the very ones he had come to rescue. And as Jesus walked the road to Calvary, as the nails pierced his flesh, as the rough wood of the cross rubbed against his broken skin, his eternal Father *turned his face away from him in judgment.*

Jesus suffered and died utterly alone, without a

single friend to help bear his burden. Indeed many of his friends *hid* to escape a similar execution. This is the Jesus we can confidently approach with our feelings of loneliness. This is the God who said to his disciples after victoriously rising from the grave and before ascending into heaven: "And behold, I am with you always, to the end of the age" (Matthew 28:20).

Fear and Anxiety

A miscarriage is often more of a process than a single event, which means that its pain and fears can last for a long time. You experience cramping or notice a little spotting. Your doctor can't find a heartbeat at your regular checkup. Without warning, you begin a grueling process of waiting—waiting to see if you will lose your baby and waiting to see if your life is about to be turned upside down with grief. Similarly, *after* a miscarriage, fear of loss threatens to eclipse the joy of each new pregnancy you are blessed with. Every day is a battle to trust God with the future of your unborn child, no matter what God's will may be. But take heart in knowing that our Savior acutely understands these battles to trust him—in the waiting and in the process of loss.

Let's take a closer look at our Savior's dark night in the garden of Gethsemane. There, while his friends slumbered, the Savior agonized alone. As he spent the night in prayer, preparing for the suffering ahead of him, we see a holy war taking place. In those frightful moments, Jesus was faced with the temptation to reject his Father's will and refuse to bear the sins of men. Indeed, the weight of mankind's destiny upon his shoulders was so great that he begged for another way, saying, "Father, if you are willing, remove this cup from me" (Luke 22:42). So intense were the emotions coursing through his veins that great drops of bloody sweat rolled down from his brow. Yet, in humble obedience, he finished his prayer with these victorious words: "Nevertheless, not my will, but yours, be done" (Luke 22:42). The road before him was far worse than any imaginable nightmare, but Jesus set his mind on his Father and therefore conquered the temptation to let fear overcome him.

The woman who has miscarried desperately needs to fellowship with her Savior in the garden. What woman would not similarly ask the Lord to remove the bitter cup of miscarriage from her? As she begins to feel the cramps signaling the loss of her baby, remembering her suffering Savior can be a precious balm to her soul, for he too was tempted to fear the road set before him. I found this account of Jesus particularly comforting as I experienced new pregnancies after my miscarriages. It was difficult to trust the Lord with the future of each new baby. Knowing that even Jesus had struggled to accept his Father's will gave me a great peace; he had come through the same temptation victoriously, so he could understand me and comfort me. Jesus faced a horrific reality and still trusted his Father, so he knows the emotions experienced by a woman who miscarries.

Intimate Loss

One of the greatest tragedies of miscarriage is the intimate nature of losing a child still within you. The unborn baby, though distinct in its humanity, is still very much a part of the mother; her body physically sustains that life, feeding and protecting the developing baby. Emotionally, she loves and cares for her unborn baby with the intensity only a parent can understand. Then suddenly, through the tragedy of miscarriage, her baby is torn from her body; the child she has loved so dearly is no longer living, the unique soul who resided within her no longer there. The separation seems beyond dreadful.

Once again, however, our Savior is well equipped to minister to us in our time of need. Dan G. McCartney says that Jesus can empathize with us in our grief over broken relationships: "God knows what it is like to suffer, not just because he sees it in far greater clarity than we, but because he has personally suffered in the most severe way possible...the disruption of his own family (the Trinity) by the immensity of his own wrath against sin."[11]

The Father, Son, and Spirit have lived as one for all eternity past. Though each is unique in personhood, they enjoy perfect, unhindered unity and fellowship as *one being*. We call this mystery the Trinity, and it is the distinct nature of the God whom Christians worship. Jesus had experienced this beautiful, mysterious relationship of oneness for all of eternity with the Father and Spirit. In John 1:18, Jesus is described as being *eternally* in the "bosom" of the Father and in John 17:24, Jesus says that the Father, "loved [him] before the foundation of the world."

No human relationship has ever known this intensity of love or this level of utter satisfaction in the fellowship of another—not even a mother in relationship to her child. Yet, what we see at the cross is the Father voluntarily giving up his beloved Son to death and judgment as well as the Son voluntarily giving up his life as a willing sacrifice to redeem his people. We see a disruption in their exquisite relationship with one another—a void where there had once been infinite blessedness.

In that holy moment when God turned his back on his beloved Son and judged him for the sins of men, John Calvin suggests that Jesus was understandably "seized with horror, which would have been sufficient to swallow up a hundred times all the men in the world."[12] Thus, the eternal Son of God cried out in misery, "My God, my God, why have you forsaken me?" (Matthew 27:46). Surely no pain of separation and loss will ever compare to the horror of that moment. This was the judgment he *voluntarily* took upon himself in order to save the souls of men. And as he cried, "It is finished," he yielded up his spirit to his Father and died as our perfect substitute. This is the God who offers his fellowship to *you*. Run to him, and find comfort where it is abounding!

To Know God and Be Like Him

Suffering is not unique to Christians, but the way in which we experience it differs greatly from the way the rest of the world does. The Bible says that we have been united to Christ in his death and resurrection (Romans 6:5, 2 Corinthians 4:10, Galatians 2:20) and that we, as his church, are members of his body (1 Corinthians 12:27, Ephesians 5:23). This unity between Jesus and his ransomed people greatly affects the way we suffer because it means that we do not suffer alone. We face loss, pain, and death as those loved and comforted by our holy Savior. Jesus tasted death (Hebrews 2:9) and experienced grief *partly for the purpose of personally sympathizing with us*. He "nourishes and cherishes" us (Ephesians 5:29) and prays for us even now (Romans 8:34). Indeed, because Christ voluntarily experienced the wrath of God on our behalf, we can experience his perfect and all-sufficient love for all of eternity.

What's more, as we suffer and experience the unique fellowship of the Son of God in our grief, our lives are being molded to more greatly resemble his, and our affections are being stirred toward greater love for him. In this way, our suffering *with* Christ makes us more *like* Christ as we behold him with greater clarity. This is the fountain from which all sanctification flows, and suffering is perfectly suited to drive us to the Good Shepherd who so lovingly suffered on behalf of his lost sheep.

* * *

A Prayer for the Suffering Mother

Loving Savior, as this beloved sister walks through the immense suffering of losing her baby, would you help her to see how deeply you love her? Would you remind her that you too have suffered the devastating effects of the fall, but that you did so in order to free her from the curse of death? Use this time of intense grief to draw her into greater fellowship with you, that she may be conformed to your image, for her great good and your great glory. I pray all these things because of your substitutionary sacrifice. Amen.

Four
HARD FROSTS AND SPRING FLOWERS

"This may be God's way of sparing you from greater pain in the future. He must have known there was something wrong with the baby." My heart burned within my chest as this friend attempted to comfort me by rationalizing away my baby's death. Her intent was good, but her words felt more like daggers than healing balm to my wounded soul.

I was stunned that she thought it would be better for our child to die than to come into this world with a disability. Our child was wanted, no matter what difficulty or pain might have accompanied his or her life. And my friend's conjecture, though conceivably true, was only one possibility in the infinitely vast and complex purposes of God. Yes, he may have taken our baby's life to spare the baby and us from greater pain in the future, but if that was *the* reason, why allow the baby to be conceived in the first place? A God who is all-knowing and sovereign over all that occurs could have simply prevented the entire pregnancy. Her simplistic rationale felt painfully inadequate as I sought to accept this difficult providence of God. Human attempts to explain his hidden purposes so often do.

Mysterious Ways

We would love to be able to fit God's inexhaustible wisdom into a neat little box, wouldn't we? Family and friends long to offer a grieving mother a specific, plausible reason why God has allowed such a painful trial to enter her life. And for the mother who has lost her baby, it feels as though a justifiable purpose would make the horror she's walking through just a little bit more bearable. More often than not, however, God doesn't reveal particular reasons for his actions.

Job, for instance, was never aware of the conversation that had taken place between God and Satan prior to his children, servants, and business being torn from him. Neither was he told that the trials he faced would result in a permanent testimony of God's supreme worth in his own life. In fact, in his infinite wisdom, when God wanted to comfort and bless Job, he didn't give him a reason for his suffering. He gave Job something far better—a reason to trust God in and through that suffering. In a stunning display of his grace, God chose to remind Job of his holy and trustworthy character.

Speaking out of the whirlwind, our majestic God overwhelmed Job with a glimpse of his magnificent nature, recounting his works of creation, his power to sustain everything he has made, and his complete control over it all. In the end, reflecting on his earlier complaints to God, Job admitted, "I have uttered what I did not understand, things too wonderful for me, which I did not know"(Job 42:3). Seeing more of the Lord's incomprehensible nature reminded Job that he was merely a creature. He had no right to question the Creator, whose wisdom is too wonderful for a human mind to comprehend. In this knowledge, Job found the peace his soul craved.

A mother grieving miscarriage can find peace in exactly the same place. She might even try singing William Cowper's hymn, "God Moves in a Mysterious Way," which beautifully articulates how the Lord's perfect wisdom moves us to trust him in the midst of painful trials:

> Deep in unfathomable mines
> Of never failing skill
> He treasures up His bright designs
> And works His sovereign will.
>
> Ye fearful saints, fresh courage take;
> The clouds ye so much dread
> Are big with mercy and shall break
> In blessings on your head.
>
> Judge not the Lord by feeble sense,
> But trust Him for His grace;
> Behind a frowning providence
> He hides a smiling face.

> His purposes will ripen fast,
> Unfolding every hour;
> The bud may have a bitter taste,
> But sweet will be the flower.

Cowper's poetry describes the difficult scriptural unity of God's "frowning providence" (how he allows terrible trials in our lives) and his hidden "smiling face" (how he desires our good). Indeed, it is often through bitter grief that God produces the sweetest fruit in our lives. So while we typically lack extensive knowledge (if any knowledge at all) of why we suffer, we *do* have the joy of knowing that we do not suffer for a moment outside of our God's perfect and loving will.

Defining "Sweet"

When Cowper says our trials produce sweet flowers, what exactly does he mean? Is this an empty platitude? What does "sweet flowers" mean to the woman who has miscarried? How could losing your baby ever produce something good? To find the answers to this question, let's look at a familiar passage of Scripture that acts as a strong foundation for Cowper's beautiful poetry:

> And we know that for those who love God *all things work together for good*, for those who are called according to his purpose. For those whom he foreknew he also predestined to be *conformed to the image of his Son*, in order that he might be the firstborn among many brothers. (Romans 8:28–29)

Notice first that this promise is only for those who love God and have been called by God. It is *not* true that all things will work together for the good of God's enemies. Only those who have placed their faith in the substitutionary work of Christ on the cross as payment for their sins can legitimately claim this promise. But God's blood-bought children can rest assured that he has not, nor will he ever, allow a single thing to come into our lives that hasn't first been sifted through his loving hands. What glorious peace can come from this knowledge!

Furthermore, Paul says we believers should *know* that all things are working together for our good. He does not say we should try to *feel* this is true, but rather that we must *trust* the revealed Word of God. This is particularly important for those going through terrible trials that *feel* altogether irredeemable.

When a Christian woman holds the tiny form of her miscarried baby, she has the great privilege of being able to ask the Holy Spirit for faith—the faith to recognize the unseen biblical and spiritual dimensions of her trial. In that tragic moment, she has a rich opportunity to lean on her Savior—trusting that even in the evil that is death, Scripture promises that her redeemer God will bring good from it. Through the pain and grief, she can endeavor to call to mind the unchanging love of Jesus. As Edith Clarkson encourages us,

> Let us learn to live the life that is hidden with Christ in God, anchored safe within the veil in the heavenly throne. Let us find there vision to see earth's suffer-

ings in the light of the sovereign Love that holds our every breath in his wounded hands, knowing that whatever he purposes in the trials he sends us, he purposes it in purest love.[13]

Lastly, from this passage we learn specifically *what* God defines as our "good." Our ultimate good is that we increasingly take on the perfect moral character of Christ. This is exactly what Cowper means by "sweet flowers." We must not miss this point, for when we understand the good that God is working toward in each of our lives, it transforms our understanding of trials and grief. This truth can bring us true *comfort* amid profound suffering, even when it seems impossible to *feel* happiness or joy.

Despite the fact that it chafes against our natural, self-centered inclinations, God is not primarily concerned with our comfort or health or material prosperity. That is not the kind of "good" he has promised us. What God has promised to his children is infinitely better: first and foremost, that we will be "conformed to the image of his Son."

In other words, God is more concerned with our ultimate holiness than he is with our temporary, emotional happiness (though, as we will see in a moment, holiness leads to happiness). This is why we can face something as terrible as miscarriage and understand that although the present pain and grief are real, God is working for our ultimate good. Trials sanctify us and draw us into closer fellowship with God, which inevitably leads to genuine, *eternal* happiness.

As true and wonderful as this is, it is nevertheless one of the great paradoxes of the Christian faith that we will all wrestle with to some degree until the day we meet the Lord face-to-face.

The Good Doctor

In his book *All Things for Good*, Thomas Watson likens God to a skilled apothecary who carefully works together poisonous ingredients in order to make a "sovereign medicine" that will produce a beneficial result in his patients.[14] This is what Paul means in Romans 8 when he says God works together "all things." He uses the blessings *and* the trials to make us holy. Indeed, *it is for this very reason that we were saved*: that he might transform us from fallen creatures into holy children of God. Just as evil men with evil intentions were used by God to bring about the salvation of men through the crucifixion of Christ, so too are the evil events of our lives subject to God's ultimate goal for us. Trials are a part of his sovereign, sanctifying will for all of his children (Romans 5:3, James 1:2).

By masterfully weaving these trials into the fabric of our lives, God is gradually returning us to the perfected state that our first parents, Adam and Eve, lost in the garden of Eden (Titus 2:14). Christians refer to this as progressive sanctification or being "made" holy. Though we are already declared holy and blameless before God, we continue to struggle against sin every day of our lives. The indwelling Holy Spirit is constantly working within us to produce a greater disdain for sin and a greater love for God; he is constantly making us more like the perfect Son. We will be fully conformed to him in heaven, but the process begins here in this world, continuing until death, as God chisels away at the old man and reveals the new.

This glorious process is often conducted under the least glorious and most unpleasant of circumstances. Losing a baby to miscarriage would certainly qualify as a "poisonous ingredient" in the mixture of providence God has ordained for us. But as Watson so eloquently writes further on in his book, "as the hard frosts in winter bring on the flowers in the spring; and as the night ushers in the morning-star: so the evils of affliction produce much good in those that love God."[15]

Does this mean God doesn't care about our present happiness? Does he ignore our pain and anguish as he allows the loss of a precious baby? Does he only have the end result of holiness in view? On the contrary, as we saw in chapter three, Scripture testifies to a God who is constantly concerned with his people, a God who sees our pain (Psalm 56:8) and understands our struggles (Isaiah 53:3, Hebrews 4:15). He is not ambivalent about our pain, but vehemently despises evil and death. Yet God knows that, to the extent our experiences of joy in this life are disconnected from fellowship with him, they will be counterfeit and fleeting. Therefore, his chief desire for us is that all our happiness be ultimately grounded in the only genuine source there is: himself. The blessing of children is profound, but the blessing of fellowship with our heavenly Father far outweighs any earthly delight we could experience in this life. As the psalmist says to God, "in your presence there is fullness of joy; at your right hand are pleasures forevermore" (Psalm 16:11). God knows this and acts accordingly.

We tend to come to God like the paralytic in Mark's gospel, convinced that our happiness is tied up in the here and now. Just as he and his friends sought physical healing, we want to be healed of disabilities and rid of our problems. When Jesus bent down toward him and joyfully proclaimed, "Son, your sins are forgiven" (Mark 2:5), he placed his initial focus on the man's spiritual health rather than his physical suffering. Jesus didn't do this to be cruel, nor to be funny. The Savior, in his infinite love, dealt first with the chief issue: damning sin. He wanted the man, and all others watching, to enjoy true fellowship with the Father. He desires the very same thing for those who walk through the trial of miscarriage. In any trial, let us seek to set our minds on the spiritual blessing he desires to lavish upon us.

Spirit, Use This

Nausea, fatigue, morning sickness, migraines, cramping, dizziness: these are all symptoms of early pregnancy that women experience in varying degrees. Hopes and dreams also accompany these physical symptoms: visions of rocking your bundle of joy to sleep, braiding the hair of your little princess, teaching your son how to throw a baseball. As the physical symptoms change your body, the promise that it will all be worth it in the end keeps you pushing forward, one cracker at a time.

Then suddenly it's all over. The visions of your child disperse like a fine mist as the ultrasound technician sneaks out the door to tell your doctor the bad news. Now you are faced with the heart-breaking thought that it has all been for nothing. The physical symptoms that have plagued you for the past couple of months have led to this, your baby's death. It can feel like such a waste. Yet, according to Romans 8, nothing from the smallest inconvenience in your day to the biggest disappointment of your life is outside the redeeming hand of God. This loss has not been for nothing, and no pregnancy is a waste. In reality, the past weeks of pregnancy—no matter how many they were—as well as the future weeks, months, and even years of sorrow, are actually meant for your good as they lead to greater Christlikeness.

The Spirit of God may choose to do this in many ways. As we close this chapter, we will look at five ways that our loving God may use your miscarriage for your spiritual good.

For Salvation

During his earthly ministry, Jesus said, "The time is fulfilled, and the kingdom of God is at hand; repent and believe in the gospel" (Mark 1:15). God calls every one of us to turn from our sins and put our trust in Jesus for salvation. Is it possible that you have never truly done this? As the profound loss of your child filters through your soul, do you find yourself wrestling with questions about God's goodness and your relationship to him?

This trial may be the gracious hand of God calling

you out of your spiritual slumber and into a genuine, saving knowledge of him. Search your heart and allow this sobering experience to reveal the substance of your faith. Have you been trusting in something other than Christ alone for your salvation—perhaps your family's faith, your good works, or your morality? No greater good could come from this tragedy than for you to turn to the Savior and seek his forgiveness for your sins. He is ready and willing to do just that.

For Communion

When all earthly joys are stripped away, we often experience a heightened sense of the presence of God in our lives. Just as you find your hearing enhanced when you sit in complete darkness, so too we can more easily appreciate and treasure God's ever-present love when the distractions of this life dissipate. In these times of suffering when the things that once filled our lives with joy are no longer available to us, we can see his fellowship for what it truly is: the sweetest of all life's blessings. As David prayed in Psalm 23:4, "Even though I walk through the valley of the shadow of death, I will fear no evil, *for you are with me*; your rod and your staff, they comfort me." As we saw in the previous chapter, the great blessing every Christian receives during trials is the heightened reality of God's presence with them.

As we fix our gaze amid painful trials upon our loving Savior, a marvelous thing happens—we become more like him. Paul tells us in 2 Corinthians 3:18 that it is in "beholding the glory of the Lord" that we "are being transformed into the same image from one degree of glory to another." In other words, as we cling tightly "to Jesus, the founder and perfecter of our faith" (Hebrews 12:2), the Holy Spirit is hard at work, bringing about our sanctification. Trials are an essential tool that God uses to conform us to the image of his Son precisely because they force us into greater Christ-dependency.

This is why the Bible often encourages us to welcome trials into our lives with joy. It isn't because they are inherently fun or pleasant, but because God is faithful to use them for our spiritual good—ridding us of sinful self-reliance and replacing it with humble trust in our sovereign God. In James 1:2–5 we are told to "count it all joy" when we experience trials because they produce steadfastness of character, which leads to spiritual maturity. Similarly, Paul calls us to,

> Rejoice in our sufferings, knowing that suffering produces endurance, and endurance produces character, and character produces hope, and hope does not put us to shame, because God's love has been poured into our hearts through the Holy Spirit who has been given to us. (Romans 5:3–5)

As we walk through the terrible trial of miscarriage, we can have confidence that our loving God will do this good work in us. We can rejoice in the knowledge that he is maturing our faith and conforming us to the image of his Son. He is teaching us to find our peace and hope in the gospel rather than in earthly blessings, and in so doing fitting our hearts and minds for heaven. Miscarriages will produce spiritual fruit (Galatians 5:22–23) in the life of a Christian woman—for her good and for the glory of God. In this, we can rejoice.

For Fellowship

A marvelous blessing that will flow from your miscarriage will be the ability to relate to other sufferers in their times of sorrow. In a world marred by sin, we have many opportunities for fellowship among the mourning, but it can be difficult to know exactly how to serve and love with sensitivity those walking through various types of grief. Personal pain and loss equips you with a heightened sensitivity to the needs of others and a precious ability to enter into their grief. A woman who experiences miscarriage will be better equipped to serve those who encounter similar loss, showing them the love and compassion of God. In this way, God equips us to bear sympathetically the burdens of fellow brothers and sisters in Christ (Galatians 6:2) and to suffer genuinely alongside them (1 Corinthians 12:26). As Paul said of his own trials, God "comforts us in all our affliction, so that we may be able to comfort those who are in any affliction, with the comfort with which we ourselves are comforted by God" (2 Corinthians 1:4).

For Testimony

Some of the most encouraging figures in the Christian faith are those who have suffered much. Their stories are memorable because their sufferings have revealed not their *own* strength, but the all-surpassing worth of the gospel of Jesus. Indeed, the way any Christian suffers can either testify to the reality of the gospel or obscure its world-altering glory. When we trust in God's goodness and sovereignty amid pain and despair, we demonstrate that something greater than our immediate circumstances matters.

This does not mean Christians should slap on a fake grin as their souls are bleeding. On the contrary, it means that we should be honest and genuine in our suffering, while simultaneously upholding the truths of God's Word. By doing so, we display God's supreme worth in our lives as well as his ability to uphold us in our weakness.

This kind of testimony serves not only as evangelism to unbelievers but as encouragement and edification to Christians. When one Christian witnesses another believer's commitment to the Lord during pain, it builds faith and prepares him or her to face the inevitable next bout of suffering more biblically and fruitfully.

Sometimes, when we suffer in a way that glorifies God, we also end up encouraging and edifying ourselves. The spiritual struggles you face during trials remind you of the reality of your faith in God and the very real presence of the Holy Spirit within you. Your struggle for joy amid grief is proof of God's good work within you, and this builds hope and endurance (1 Peter 1:7).

There is another way in which the suffering of miscarriage in particular can be a testimony to a watching world: by testifying to the dignity and worth of every human life. Your grief over the death of your baby (whom much of the world would classify as mere "tissue") is a powerful corrective to a culture that throws away the lives of their children when they are considered inconvenient. Your baby, like every other child conceived, was made in God's image and deserves to be loved and mourned. Your suffering testifies to this.

For Perspective

Experiencing the death of a loved one can loosen our ties to this world like little else can. The Bible refers to Christians as "sojourners and exiles" in this world (1 Peter 2:11). When death, the dark evil that separates spirit from body, is experienced in such an intimate way, these terms take on new significance. Knowing that your baby is no longer with you, but rather with God, makes the reality of heaven all the more tangible. You learn more acutely what it is to live between the two worlds of the seen and the unseen. You long to be free from your present body of death and to walk in perfection with your Savior. You long for heaven.

This is a good gift from God. It allows us to gain perspective on this life. Our lives on this earth are a mist, appearing and then all too quickly vanishing (James 4:14). The good and joyful gifts of grace that we partake of in this fleeting life, as well as the trials and sorrows we encounter, will be instantly overshadowed by the coming joy that awaits us for all of eternity. This is the vision every Christian is called to have as we walk through life, and painful trials like miscarriage are a means by which God can effectively direct our gaze toward our eternal future with him

Seek His Enabling Power

Miscarriage is painful, both physically and emotionally. Denying this reality is futile. Instead, we must confirm the horror and pain of what has happened, while at the same time humbly thanking God for his ability to produce joy from sorrow—to produce sweet flowers from winter's frosts. As you journey through the waves of grief brought on by the loss of your baby, ask our good and loving heavenly Father to use this dark time for your spiritual good. This sorrow isn't without purpose, but it is only through the enabling power of the Holy Spirit at work within you that your mourning can be transformed into rejoicing.

* * *

A Prayer for the Suffering Mother

Loving Father, you are the great physician of our souls. In love, you use every trial that comes into our lives to conform us to the image of your Son. Because we know that you are sovereign, and because we know that you are good, we can have confidence that you will not allow any pain to come into our lives without purpose. Through your Word we know that you use all things for our good. Therefore, would you encourage this sister in Christ, with the knowledge that her miscarriage is a part of your gracious plan for her? Though the loss of her baby is incredibly painful, would you allow her to see the good things that you are bringing out of it? Holy Spirit, would you use this trial to sanctify her and draw her nearer her Savior and into greater conformity to his image. In his name I ask these things. Amen.

Five
THE COMING GLORY

When our second miscarriage took place, I was well into the second trimester of my pregnancy. Our baby girl was about the size of my hand—tiny, yet marvelously formed and extremely precious. Because of her gestational age, we decided to induce labor. We were then left with the difficult decision of what to do with her little body once she arrived. She was big enough to bury, but we were not legally required to do so in a cemetery. After some consideration, we decided to bury her under a tree on my parents' land where we'd carved our initials while we were dating. The horrible question remained, however, of what we would take her home from the hospital in.

So the night before my induction, we found ourselves walking through the florescent-lit isles of a craft store. We were searching for some kind of box beautiful enough to express the love we had for our daughter, while at the same time fighting our utter repulsion toward placing her precious body in a common household knickknack. As I wrapped my sweater around my pregnant belly, the horror of what was scheduled for the next day brought tears to my eyes. Probably nobody else in that store could have imagined what we had come there to do.

After I delivered our daughter, we made the four-hour trip to my parents' home. The wooden box we'd chosen sat on the floorboard of our car. The delicate flowers that decorated its lid whispered of the treasure within: the body of our first daughter. We spent those four painful hours discussing what we wanted to name her. Though we'd always dreamt of naming a girl, it seemed difficult to find the perfect name when so much of our daughter's existence was now associated with pain and heartbreak. As I scrolled through lists of names on my phone, nothing seemed appropriate until I stumbled upon the name "Anastasia." It means "resurrection," and I knew it was perfect.

Suffering and Glory

It has been my goal, in this little book, to help you see the unique trial of miscarriage within the broader context of God's redemptive plan. In other words, I've endeavored to show how miscarriage relates to the gospel. This is because I truly believe that healing and joy after miscarriage can only flow out of knowing our great God and how the loss of a child relates to him.

So far, we've seen how death and sorrow entered our world through Adam and Eve, how God has reigned sovereignly over his creation to bring about the salvation of mankind, and how our Savior took on the weak and humble nature of humanity so that he could be a worthy substitute for us upon the cross. All along the journey, we've marveled at the way God uses the terrible effects of the fall to sanctify his people, further his redemptive plan, and bring glory to his name.

Most specifically, we've seen how miscarriage is so much more than the painful loss of a precious baby. Miscarriage is a part of the narrative of God's people; it is a part of God's *gospel story*. This means that we are all a part of something much bigger than ourselves. The times of sadness we face place us right in the middle of the bigger story of God's people. Thankfully, though, suffering is not how the gospel story ends. Suffering may be our current reality, but it is not our future reality.

In his book *The Glory of Christ*, John Owen says, "So much as we know of Christ, his sufferings and his glory, so much do we understand of the Scripture and no more."[16] This is because all of Scripture points us to a Savior who would *first* suffer to redeem his people and then *later* receive the glory due to his name (Hebrews 2:9). We must keep these two paradoxical experiences of Christ, and the order in which they occur, at the forefront of our minds when we walk through trials. For we, who are united to Christ, must also experience pain and sorrow in this sin-infected world *before* entering into the glory he purchased for us on the cross. But because we *are* united to Christ, we look forward to a glorious *future* yet to come. It is the hope of this future glory that allows us to humbly endure the suffering we now face, just as the joy set before Christ motivated him to endure the agonies of the cross (Hebrews 12:2).

A Sure Hope

When we talk about our future hope, we must differentiate between biblical, faith-fueled hope and hopeful *wishing*. In today's culture, the term "hope" often refers to something that you are not entirely sure will come to pass, but *wish* for. In this sense, most people *hope* that they will enter into heaven when they die, but rarely do they *know* they will. In contrast, Christians cling to a hope securely built upon the factual resurrection of our Lord and Savior Jesus Christ. In fact, Jesus' resurrection is so foundational to our faith that Paul says without it we are to be pitied (1 Corinthians 15:12–19). Unless Jesus actually rose from the dead as he said he would, we've placed our faith in a mere man whose body decayed ages ago in a tomb outside of Jerusalem. If that were true, the best we could look forward to after the sufferings we experience in this life would be a similar rotting fate.

The wonderful reality in which Christians live is the reality of Jesus' true, physical, historical, eye-witnessed, factual resurrection (Acts 13:30; 26:15–18; 1 Corinthians 15:6). And this monumental event completes our salvation (Romans 4:25). Because Jesus rose, we too can look forward to a day when we will be raised from the dead (1 Corinthians 15:20–22), freed from sin and its horrid effects. Our hope is based on this one great accomplishment.

This is why the sting of death, in all its horror, is but

light and momentary. As 2 Timothy 1:10 tells us, our victorious Savior "abolished death and brought life and immortality to light through the gospel." He died but *now* lives forevermore, authoritatively carrying the keys to Death and Hades in his hand as we do the keys to our car (Revelation 1:18). No sorrow we encounter in this life can be so great as to shake the surety of our future joy, for it is held firm in the grip of our triumphant, risen King.

Our Future

The surety of our future hope lets us walk confidently through this life's various trials because it promises something better just around the corner. But it is the *substance* of that future hope that makes even the most difficult trials bearable. In Romans 8:18, Paul writes that "the sufferings of this present time are not worth comparing with the glory that is to be revealed to us." What exactly is this glory and how does it transform our current sorrow?

Paul tells us more about that glory in the next verses: as we considered earlier in this book, we look forward to the redemption of our bodies (v 23). Notice where Jesus pointed the hearts of his disciples when, on the night of his betrayal, he foretold his death to them once more:

> Let not your hearts be troubled. Believe in God; believe also in me. In my Father's house are many rooms. If it were not so, would I have told you that *I go to prepare a place for you*? And if I go and prepare

a place for you, *I will come again and will take you to myself*, that where I am you may be also (John 14:1–4).

Jesus' words are the same to us, for we are living in an age of waiting. Jesus has come to Earth, paid the penalty for our sins, and ascended into heaven, where he now sits at the right hand of God the Father. We, who have placed our trust in him for salvation, anxiously await the day when he will return for us, just as he predicted that night more than 2,000 years ago, redeeming our fallen, mortal bodies and sanctifying us fully, never to sin again. For the substance of our future joy is wrapped up in the promise that where he is, we will also be; that as he has risen, so too shall we rise. Paul describes Christ's return and our resurrection in 1 Thessalonians 4:16–17:

> For the Lord himself will descend from heaven with a cry of command, with the voice of an archangel, and with the sound of the trumpet of God. And the dead in Christ will rise first. Then we who are alive, who are left, will be caught up together with them in the clouds to meet the Lord in the air, and so we will always be with the Lord.

In that day we will receive blessings upon blessings, but there are two specific aspects of our resurrection that I wish to emphasize, as they contain particular hope for those who have suffered from miscarriage.

The first is that we will be transformed through the power of Christ's blood into his very likeness. The apostle John wrote of our coming transformation when he said, "we know that when he appears we shall be like him, because we shall see him as he is" (1 John 3:2). In this life, we experience the pain of living in bodies of death. Women who miscarry have experienced the horror of a member of the human race dying *within* them. But in the resurrection we will no longer be subjected to the sin-marred bodies we've inherited from Adam. Instead, we will inherit new, glorified bodies made in the image of the resurrected Jesus (1 Corinthians 15:49). We will be pure and spotless in every way—just as our Creator always intended. Death and pain will be no more because sin will be no more.

A second great blessing we will experience in that day will be the unhindered fellowship of our Savior. Without the barrier of sin between us, we will finally be free to enjoy his abounding love in unceasing waves of grace. The pain we have experienced in this life will be swept away as the tide of his comfort swells. We are told in Revelation 21:3–4 that in the resurrection, "the dwelling place of God is with man," and his presence is the ultimate comfort: "He will wipe away every tear from their eyes, and death shall be no more, neither shall there be mourning, nor crying, nor pain anymore, for the former things have passed away."

Is it any wonder that Jesus defined eternal life as *knowing* him (John 17:3)? As we suffer in this life, we look forward to an eternity in the presence of our loving and compassionate God—a presence so glorious that it banishes darkness for all time (Revelation 22:5). The tears we've cried over our empty wombs will be gently wiped away by his nail-pierced hands, and in their place he will substitute the blush of eternal joy.

Their Present

But what about the dear children we've lost? Every mother who has ever lost a baby is plagued by the question of where her child's soul is now. We desire above all else to know that our babies are in heaven with the Lord, but we may fear putting our faith in emotions rather than the authoritative Word of God. A careful study of Scripture will not only put these fears to rest but also provide great peace and hope to parents who have been temporarily parted from their child.

We must, of course, affirm that Scripture teaches that babies are not inherently worthy of salvation. We know from the Word of God that every member of the human race is conceived with a sin nature. As children of Adam and Eve, we are *all* naturally bent toward rebellion. In Romans 5:12 we are told that "sin came into the world through one man, and death through sin, and so death spread to *all men* because all sinned" and in Psalm 51:5, David writes, "Behold, I was brought forth in iniquity, and in sin did my mother conceive me." These passages highlight the biblical teaching that every member of the human race inherits a sin nature from our first parents, Adam and Eve.

Because unborn children are members of the human

race, they immediately need a Savior upon conception.
But miscarried children do not have the opportunity
to express faith in Jesus for salvation. This leaves us to
wonder whether they will be punished for their inherited
sin *natures*, even though they have never *willfully* sinned.

Two specific passages in the Bible seem to refute
the possibility of babies suffering punishment for their
inherited sin natures. The first is Revelation 20:11–15,
where we are transported to the future judgment day
before the great white throne. It is there that all men
and women are judged according to "what they had
done." On that day, "if anyone name was not found
written in the book of life, he was thrown into the lake
of fire." What we see in this description of the judgment
day is that the *act* of sinning, rather than the condition of
being a sinner, is what ultimately condemns a person and
consigns them to hell. In regard to this argument, John
MacArthur says,

> Scripture teaches that we are *saved* by grace, but we
> are *damned* by works. Scripture teaches that eternal
> punishment is the wage due those who have willfully
> sinned. Nowhere in the Bible is anyone ever threat-
> ened with hell merely for the guilt inherited from
> Adam. Instead, whenever Scripture describes the
> inhabitants of hell, the stress is on their *willful* acts
> of sin and rebellion (1 Corinthians 6:9–10, Galatians
> 5:19–21, Ephesians 5:5, Colossians 3:6, Revelation 21:8
> and 22:15). Scripture always connects eternal condem-
> nation with works of unrighteousness—willful sin.[17]

Babies have no ability to willfully sin and thus have nothing for our holy God to judge. If they were condemned to hell, they would be receiving punishment for sins never committed, which would be unjust and contrary to the very nature of our God.

The second passage of Scripture that seems to refute the notion that babies who die will receive punishment for their sin natures is Romans 1:18–20:

> For the wrath of God is revealed from heaven against all ungodliness and unrighteousness of men, who by their unrighteousness suppress the truth. For what can be known about God is plain to them, because God has shown it to them. *For his invisible attributes, namely, his eternal power and divine nature, have been clearly perceived, ever since the creation of the world, in the things that have been made. So they are without excuse.*

In this passage, Paul argues that every person is held accountable to God for the knowledge expressed about him through creation. Humanity is "without excuse" for failing to honor God as God, because he has clearly revealed himself through the visible world. As the psalmist proclaims, "The heavens declare the glory of God, and the sky above proclaims his handiwork" (Psalm 19:1).

Obviously, babies do not have the mental capacity to see the creation and know that there is a Creator to thank for it. They are not "suppressing the truth," as Romans condemns, because they are not capable of *understanding* the truth. Therefore, according to this passage, it would seem that babies actually *have* an excuse and cannot be condemned by a just God.[18]

Beyond these two passages, Scripture seems to uniformly agree that babies who die are instantly transported to paradise with God. For instance, when David's baby son conceived in adultery dies as a consequence of David's sin, the king's counselors are confused as to why the king no longer fasts and prays and mourns over his child. David confidently replies to them,

> While the child was still alive, I fasted and wept, for I said, "Who knows whether the LORD will be gracious to me, that the child may live?" But now he is dead. Why should I fast? Can I bring him back again? *I shall go to him, but he will not return to me.*" (2 Samuel 12:22–23)

David was clearly not suggesting that he would join his son in hell one day, but rather expressed his peace in the knowledge that one day he would join his son in heaven.

Similarly, in a dark passage expressing great anguish, Job assumes that all infants who die are saved (Job 3:11–19). Job sincerely believed that dying as a baby would have been better for him than experiencing the trials he was walking through. After all, the "place of rest" he described for these babies was clearly not a place of torment but of peace. The author of Ecclesiastes shares this opinion, claiming that it would be better to be a stillborn child than to live as an unsatisfied man (Ecclesiastes 6:3–6). He must assume that such babies enjoy peace, making it truly desirable for a man to die at his birth rather than live an ungrateful and godless life.

These three passages of Scripture imply that children who die in infancy receive special grace from our Lord, a grace that allows them to be saved through Christ's sacrifice without ever willfully expressing faith in the gospel themselves. Just as John the Baptist was *filled with the Holy Spirit while yet in his mother's womb* and unable to express faith in Christ, so too the eternal destiny of miscarried babies must be, as B. B. Warfield wrote, "determined irrespective of their choice, by an unconditional decree of God…and their salvation is wrought by…the grace of Christ to their souls, through the immediate and irresistible operation of the Holy Spirit."[19] It is only by the marvelous grace of our loving God that our babies will join us in heaven, just as it is by grace that we will make it there ourselves.

Could there be any thought more comforting to the mother who has miscarried than that of her loving and kind Savior gathering the little children to himself in his kingdom just as he did during his time on this earth? For he himself said, "Let the little children come to me and do not hinder them, for *to such belongs the kingdom of heaven*" (Matthew 19:14).

All that is true for us in the future is true for miscarried babies in the present. Just imagine: the baby lost in miscarriage, now at this very moment alive in the truest

sense — more alive than we are! They enjoy perfections
we cannot imagine, free from ever suffering in a world
and body marred by sin. They worship and adore the
Lord freely without the weight of a rebellious nature to
hamper them. Imagine the multitude of souls — babies
who have died in the womb — who have been *chosen* by
God for the glorious light of heaven before they had the
chance to see the light of our sin-darkened world. Does
this knowledge of their resurrection not lessen the grief
we experience at *our* loss (1 Thessalonians 4:13–14)? It
must, for as Elizabeth Prentiss so beautifully penned:

> Blessed the souls that ne'er shall know
> > Of sin the mortal taint,
> The hearts that ne'er shall swell with grief
> > Or utter a complaint!
>
> Brief pangs for us, long joy for them!
> > Thy holy Name we bless,
> We could not give them up to Thee,
> > Lord, if we loved them less![20]

In a way, then, it is even more desirable than living
this life. This is what Charles Spurgeon wrote when
articulating his belief that infants who die are among
the elect of God: "We look to this as being the means
by which Christ shall see of the travail of his soul to
a great degree, and we do sometimes hope that thus
the multitude of the saved shall be made to exceed the
multitude of the *lost*."[21]

Is this not a happy thought? Do you not look forward to the day when we will join our lost babies in worshipping our King? Together we will make up a great and glorious congregation of humanity freed from the curse of sin, bowing down in the grateful adoration of our loving and victorious God. In that day, Jesus will remember the anguish of his soul as he experienced the wrath of God on our behalf, and he will be utterly satisfied (Isaiah 53:11). In that day, our Savior will receive his reward.

Fight the Battle

Until that day, we who remain in the flesh must worship through faith rather than sight, which means we must constantly be engaging in spiritual warfare as we seek to cling to the promise of our future hope.

One of the most unlikely and powerful weapons we are given in this war of faith is the weapon of corporate worship. As we gather each Sunday to lift our voices as one in praise of our Savior, we testify loudly to the truthfulness of the gospel message, both to the world *and* to one another. In his book *Gospel Formed*, J. A. Medders recalls a time when he became astutely aware of the powerful nature of singing together as one body:

> The gathered saints of a risen Galilean, the King of kings, were singing, exalting, and enjoying the gospel of the kingdom. As we sang the beautiful truths of the gospel, we were doing more than reciting words. This was no mere singing—pagans can sing. We were

engaging in exaltational exorcism. We were pushing back the darkness around us in our minds, in our hearts, and in the air."[22]

I couldn't agree more. Every Sunday, as I sing along with my brothers and sisters in Christ, my mind instinctively turns to the different struggles members of my church are going through. I watch them sing, often through tears, about the glorious God who came to earth to shed his blood for our sin. I am instantly reminded of the battle we each wage—the battle to live as citizens of a heavenly kingdom while still experiencing the trials of an earthly one.

I recall one particular Sunday when my dear friend Krista returned to church after losing her twins in a miscarriage. I knew the morning would be extremely difficult for her as she navigated the emotions surely surging through her heart. As the time of worship began, I held her hand, and we tearfully praised our Savior together. We had both experienced the heartbreaking sting of death, but at the same time we were women who had experienced the healing balm of the Lord of Life. In that moment we testified to one another of God's power and worth; we reminded one another of the hope we have amid loss. We were indeed participating in "exaltational exorcism."

Christians are never free from battling the darkness in this life. We cannot escape the pain and suffering we encounter. Never imagine there is some higher spiritual realm where the *really* godly Christians live unaffected by their pain. Instead, we must recognize our weakness and constantly turn to the only physician able to heal us in our times of malady. This is why in 1 Peter believers aren't encouraged to deny the suffering they face, but rather to rejoice in the gospel, even if "for a little while, if necessary, [we are] grieved by various trials" (1 Peter 1:6).

We feel real suffering, but in the context of eternity, it lasts only "a little while." Therefore, we have much reason to rejoice even during a terrible trial like miscarriage. Peter explained why in the verses just before his observation about grief:

> According to [God's] great mercy, he has caused us to be born again to a *living hope* through the resurrection of Jesus Christ from the dead, to an inheritance that is *imperishable*, *undefiled*, and *unfading*, *kept in heaven for you*, who by God's power are being guarded through faith for a salvation ready to be revealed in the last time. (1 Peter 1:3–4)

The key is not to *escape* the grief that miscarriage brings, but to drive our souls into the shelter of Jesus' gospel *during* that sorrow. In this way, as we remind ourselves over and over of the glory that is ours in Christ Jesus, the light of his gospel will eclipse the darkness of death that has visited our wombs. The suffering we face presently will be overshadowed by the glorious inheritance yet to come. This is a battle we fight through faith. And as we fight, experiencing glimmers of our eternal reality along the way, our souls will be happy in Jesus.

* * *

Every heart knows its own bitterness, and every heart has bitterness to know. Sin must bring sorrow, tears are the inheritance of earth's children; but in the city to which we are going, "God shall wipe away all tears from their eyes; and there shall be no more death, neither sorrow, nor crying, neither shall there be any more pain; for the former things are passed away."

Blessed be your dear name, O Lord, for this "strong consolation"—this "good hope through grace." Tears may, and must come; but if they gather in the eyes that are constantly looking up to you and heaven, they will glisten with the brightness of the coming glory.

—Susannah Spurgeon[23]

* * *

A Prayer for the Suffering Mother

Victorious King, we are in awe of the glory you have reserved for us in the resurrection. We know that we are unworthy of such grace and such mercy and look forward to praising your name for all of eternity because of it. But compassionate Savior, our lives until then are filled with such pain and such sorrow. We are weak and frail creatures who find it easy to forget our future hope and become overwhelmed by our current suffering. Would you teach us to engage in exaltational exorcism each and every day? Would you be with this dear sister in Christ who is fighting to have faith in the unseen this very moment? Teach her to lift her eyes to you, even as they are filled with tears. May your overwhelming love and goodness eclipse the darkness brought on by her miscarriage and may she find that because of this trial she has come to treasure you more. It's in your glorious name we pray. Amen.

Endnotes

1. J. I. Packer, *Knowing God* (Downers Grove, IL: InterVarsity, 1973), 24–25.
2. Heidi Murkoff and Arlene Eisenberg, *What to Expect When You're Expecting*, 3rd ed. (NewYork: Workman Publishing, 2002), xxi.
3. Susannah Spurgeon and Charles Ray, *Susannah Spurgeon: Free Grace and Dying Love* (Edinburgh: Banner of Truth Trust, 2006), 30.
4. The doctrine of common grace teaches that God, in his mercy, extends amazing grace, mercy, and blessing even to unbelievers, even those who he knows will never turn to him in faith. He does this as a constant demonstration of his compassion and willingness to forgive.
5. D. A. Carson, *How Long, Oh Lord?* (Grand Rapids, MI: Baker Academic, 2006), 44.
6. Timothy Keller, *Walking with God through Pain and Suffering* (NewYork: Dutton, 2013), 136: "When he approaches the tomb, most translations say he was 'once more deeply moved' or 'he groaned in himself" (v 38). But these translations are too weak. The Greek word used by the gospel writer John means 'to bellow with anger.'"
7. Spurgeon and Ray, *Susannah Spurgeon,* 31.
8. "Blessed Be Your Name," written by Beth Redman and Matt Redman, copyright 2002 ThankYou Music (PRS) (adm. Worldwide at CapitolCMGPublishing.com excluding Europe which is adm. by IntegrityMusic.com) Int'l copyright secured. All rights reserved. Used by permission.
9. Philip P. Bliss, *Man of Sorrows-What a Name.*
10. John Henry Newman and Maurice Francis Egan, *The Dream of Gerontius.*(NewYork: Longmans, Green, 1903), quoted in Alistair Begg and Sinclair B. Ferguson, *Name above All Names* (Wheaton, IL: Crossway, 2013), 27.
11. Dan McCartney, *Why Does It Have to Hurt?: The Meaning of Christian Suffering* (Phillipsburg, NJ: P&R, 1998), 57.
12. John Calvin and William Pringle, *Commentary on a Harmony of the Evangelists, Matthew, Mark, and Luke: VolumeThird* (Grand Rapids, MI: Baker, 2003), 319.
13. Edith Margaret Clarkson, *Grace Grows Best in Winter: Help for Those Who Must Suffer* (Grand Rapids, MI: Eerdmans, 1985), 41

(emphasis mine).

14. Thomas Watson, *All Things for Good* (Edinburgh: Banner of Truth Trust, 1986), 11.
15. Ibid., 27.
16. John Owen, *The Glory of Christ: His Office and Grace* (Fearn, Scotland: Christian Focus, 2008), 123.
17. John MacArthur, *Safe in the Arms of God: Truth from Heaven about the Death of a Child* (Nashville, TN: Thomas Nelson, 2003), 80.
18. John Piper, "Why Do You Believe That Infants Who Die Go to Heaven?" *Desiring God*, January 30, 2008, http://www.desiringgod.org/interviews/why-do-you-believe-that-infants-who-die-go-to-heaven.
19. Loraine Boettner, *The Reformed Doctrine of Predestination* (Phillipsburng, NJ: P&R, 1992), 142, quoted in MacArthur, *Safe in the Arms of God*, 78.
20. Elizabeth Prentiss, Golden Hours: "The Mother," *Hymns and Songs of the Christian Life* (New York: Anson D. F. Randolph and Company, 1874), 150.
21. Charles Spurgeon, "Expositions of the Doctrines of Grace," *Metropolitan Tabernacle Pulpit,* vol. 7 (London: Passmore and Alabaster, 1862), 300, quoted in MacArthur, *Safe in the Arms of God*, 76.
22. J. A. Medders, *Gospel Formed: Living a Grace-Addicted, Truth -Filled, Jesus-Exalting Life* (Grand Rapids, MI: Kregel, 2014), 59.
23. Spurgeon and Ray, *Susannah Spurgeon*. 30–31.

Grieving, Hope, and Solace
When a Loved One Dies in Christ

by Albert N. Martin

There is comfort for the grief. There are answers to the questions. The Bible does offer hope, solace, healing, and confidence.

Pastor Albert Martin has been there.

bit.ly/GriefHope

"This tender book by a much-loved pastor, written after the death of his beloved wife, offers comfort to those in tears. A rare guidebook to teach us how to grieve with godliness, it is relevant to us all — if not for today, then no doubt for tomorrow."
Maurice Roberts, former editor, **Banner of Truth** *magazine*

"Albert N. Martin is a seasoned pastor, skilled teacher, and gifted writer who has given us a priceless treasure in this book. All who read these pages will, unquestionably, be pointed to Christ and find themselves greatly helped."
Steve Lawson, Christ Fellowship Baptist Church, Mobile, AL

"Like turning the corner and being met by a glorious moonrise, or discovering a painter or musician who touches us in the deepest recesses of our being—this little book by Pastor Al Martin has been such an experience for me. Whether you are a pastor or counselor, one who is experiencing the pangs of grief, or a member of the church who wants to be useful to others, you need to read this book."
Joseph Pipa, President, Greenville Presbyterian Theo. Sem.

"Personal tenderness and biblical teaching in a sweet book of comfort. Buy it and give it away, but make sure to get a copy for yourself."
Dr. Joel R. Beeke, President, Puritan Reformed Theo. Sem.

JOY! – A Bible Study on
Philippians for Women

bit.ly/JoyStudy

FAITH: A Bible Study on
James for Women

bit.ly/FaithStudy

Inductive Bible studies for women by Keri Folmar
endorsed by...

Kathleen Nielson is author of the *Living Word Bible Studies*; Director of Women's Initiatives, The Gospel Coalition; and wife of Niel, who served as President of Covenant College from 2002 to 2012.

Diane Schreiner – wife of professor, author, and pastor Tom Schreiner, and mother of four grown children – has led women's Bible studies for more than 20 years.

Connie Dever is author of *The Praise Factory* children's ministry curriculum and wife of Pastor Mark Dever, President of 9 Marks Ministries

Kristie Anyabwile, holds a history degree from NC State University, and is married to Thabiti, Senior Pastor of First Baptist Church, Grand Cayman, and a Council Member for The Gospel Coalition.

Gloria Furman is a pastor's wife in the Middle East and author of *Glimpses of Grace* and *Treasuring Christ When Your Hands Are Full*.

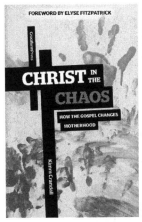

Christ in the Chaos
How the Gospel Changes Motherhood

by Kimm Crandall

MOMS: Stop comparing yourself to others. Stop striving to meet false expectations. Stop thinking your performance dictates your worth.

Look to the gospel for rest, joy, sufficiency, identity, and motivation.

bit.ly/ChristIn

"Although Kimm Crandall's message would revive any soul long-ing for the breath of the gospel of grace, I am especially eager to recommend this book to that heart who strives to know God and to make him known to the little ones who call her 'Momma.' Kimm is a candid and gracious fellow sojourner, faithfully pointing to God's immeasurable steadfast love and grace in the midst of our mess."
Lauren Chandler, wife of Matt Chandler (pastor of The Village Church), mother of three, writer, singer, and speaker

"What an amazingly wild and wise, disruptive and delighting, freeing and focusing book. Kimm's book is for every parent willing to take the stewardship of children and the riches of the gospel seriously. This is one of the most helpful and encouraging books on parenting I've read in the past twenty years. This will be a book you will want to give to parents, to-be parents, and grandparents."
Scotty Smith, author; Founding Pastor, Christ Community Church

"Kimm Crandall has discovered that chaos can be the perfect context in which to experience God's liberating grace. She is a wise, practical, gospel-drenched guide for anyone navigating through the weari-some terrain of parenting."
Tullian Tchividjian, author; Pastor, Coral Ridge Presbyterian Church

After They are Yours
The Grace and Grit of Adoption

by Brian Borgman
Foreword by Dan Cruver

This is about the "other side" of adoption, the difficult realities that are not often discussed. What do you do when it's hard to hope? Here is a story of adoption that's real, raw, redemptive, and edifying.

102 pages
bit.ly/AfterThey

"A compelling story about saying *yes* to God and then watching the Father shape and redeem his sons and daughters through love, grace, and mercy."
Kelly Rosati, V.P. Community Outreach, Focus on the Family

"The decision to adopt is heroic. The reality is often hard. This book does not sugar coat the sacrifice that comes standard with adoption. It will help those considering adoption count the cost. And it will provide encouragement and help for parents who have already welcomed a child into their forever family."
Bob Lepine, Co-Host, FamilyLife Today

"It's all here – joy, hurt, and longing. And this is precisely what we most need: truth-telling that plunges beyond cliche and facade to speak of both the beauty and the brokenness that so often come woven together in adoption, all of it wrapped round by God's limitless grace."
Jedd Medefind, President, Christian Alliance for Orphans

"Brian Borgman lets us step into his family's experience as he unashamedly shares the joys and difficulties of their adoption story. Pain and loss are an inescapable part of every adoption, and Borgman points us to the gospel that provides both the framework and the fuel families will need for the challenges... an excellent resource."
Stephen Story, Executive Director of Covenant Care Services